Redditch At War

Redditch At War

by Alan Foxall and Ray Saunders

Redditch
Advertiser

DB
PUBLISHING

3rd Battalion Worcester Volunteer Regiment at Easemoor Road Barracks, Redditch, October 1918.

First published in Great Britain in 2004 by
The Breedon Books Publishing Company Limited
Breedon House, 3 The Parker Centre,
Derby, DE21 4SZ.

This paperback edition published in Great Britain in 2013 by DB Publishing,
an imprint of JMD Media Ltd

ISBN 978-1-78091-348-3

Printed and bound in the UK by Copytech (UK) Ltd Peterborough

Contents

Dedication

We respectfully dedicate this book to the
memory of those
men and women of Redditch and District who
gave their lives in both World Wars.

Acknowledgements

This book is about Redditch folk in wartime and much of the material contained within comes from the collective archive of the authors with additional photography by Alan Foxall. It was felt however, that there must be many images of the period in family archives that could add considerably to the local interest of the book. An example of this is the search for pictures of bomb damage sustained by the town in 1940, as there are apparently none in the public domain at the present time. As a result of appeals through the local press and radio, many fine images, mainly of the two World Wars, have emerged and are contained within.

Unfortunately some names of contributors were not recorded at the time but the authors would like to thank them and the following people: Paul Betterton, Maurice Clarke, Mrs Joyce Cole, Brian Danks, Philip Davis, Phyllis Dixon, John Ellis, Mr and Mrs Garner, Philip Hunt, Mr and Mrs Ingram, Philip Jarvis, Dr Lyn Layton, Mr and Mrs J. Lewis, Heather and Julian Lloyd, Norman Neasom, Neil Partridge, Bill Preece, Barbara Ralph, John Rattue, Sid Reynolds, Maureen Saunders, Ron and Beryl Smith, Graham Stanton, Theresa Twilton, Gary Whitley and Mike Wojczynski.

Introduction

THIS BOOK is not about World War One trench warfare or 'dog fights' in the skies during World War Two but is designed to give a flavour of how the ordinary folk of Redditch coped with the enormous social upheaval caused by war and what daily life was like in the town, particularly during World War Two when, of necessity, there was more regimentation, documentation and control of the workforce and of the civilian population than ever before. Where and when you travelled was questioned. Posters asked 'Is your journey really necessary?' What and how much you ate was controlled by 'U' boats and ration books.

The social life of the town often revolved around the group you belonged to in the workplace or after work, performing duties such as Air Raid Wardens, Special Constables, Works Fire Brigades, Home Guard, etc. Although food was in short supply events such as the 'Annual Dinner' raised spirits and morale. Having the determination to defeat a common enemy gave everyone a sense of purpose and community. The book also covers the celebrations when peace was restored and the memorials to those who did not return. The identities of some of the World War One casualties are given, particularly those printed in the local newspaper, the *Redditch Indicator*. However, we have refrained from doing the same for World War Two as the printing of casualty lists for the bombing raids on Redditch in 1940 could bring painful memories to some of the older inhabitants of the town.

War came – in the form of Civil War – to the area when Redditch barely existed as a town and little is known of its involvement in the conflict. What is recorded is the fact that Redditch, along with Beoley, Hanbury, Alvechurch, Bromsgrove and other small towns and villages had to provide money and goods for the upkeep of the Royalist garrison at Worcester. However, the existence of Parliamentary committees controlling nearby Warwickshire meant that tribute was extracted from this area by both sides to the great distress and deprivation of the local population.

The Sheldons of Beoley suffered great losses. They defended Beoley Hall and Beoley Manor for the King but the Manor was destroyed on 1 April 1643 during an action against the Parliamentary forces and in December of the same year Beoley Hall was razed to

Cookhill Priory.

8

the ground on the advice of Prince Rupert 'lest the enemy should make a lodgment there'.

In November 1643 the home of the Catholic Throckmorton family, Coughton Court, was taken over by a Parliamentary force from the garrison at Warwick. In 1642 there were 35 Recusants (i.e. Catholics) in Redditch and Tardebigge, probably due to the influence of the Windsors at Hewell. Lord and Lady Windsor of Hewell Grange, Tardebigge were Catholic and Royalist. The Cookes of Bentley were a divided family – William Cookes of Norgrove Court being Catholic while Thomas Cookes of Bentley Manor was a member of the Worcestershire Parliamentary Committee.

On 9 May 1645, King Charles, accompanied by his personal lifeguard, is thought to have spent the night at Cookhill Priory. He was welcomed by William Fortescue, Lord of the Manor and owner of Cookhill Priory, and his son John, an ardent local Royalist commander. The next day the King continued on to Inkberrow. A reminder of those troubled days was discovered at Cookhill Priory some 120 years later when in 1765 a portrait of Charles I was found behind a double panelling in a room at the north end of the house.

In 1651, two years after Charles I was beheaded, Charles's son returned from exile in France and raised an army that was defeated at the Battle of Worcester. Charles II is believed to have passed through the area on his flight from Bromsgrove to Wootton Wawen. The following account appeared in a Worcester newspaper in 1874.

After the Battle of Worcester a small party of fugitives sought shelter at Hewell Grange but

Prince Rupert.

Charles I.

Lord Windsor did not think it safe to receive them in his own house. He therefore sent them to Lownes Hill where they were entertained for the night by the tenant Spencer. When they left in the morning, one of the farm men felt sure he recognised the King amongst the Cavaliers.

The 1888 *Redditch Needle District Almanac and Trades Directory* quotes in the Crabbs Cross section: 'May 1643: Charles I reviewed 10,000 men at Crabbe Crosse.' The men of Redditch have fought in most of the famous battles in recent British history. A good example being local legend Timothy Munslow who is reputed to have shod the

Duke of Wellington's horse before the Battle of Waterloo where Napoleon was finally defeated in 1815. In the same battle Tom Bright of Headless Cross was killed and William Steel of Redditch was wounded – Jack Wall, James Bayliss and Charles Avery returned home safely.

Another local soldier, Joseph Mason of Crabbs Cross, was a Corporal in the Welsh Fusiliers having joined them in 1846. He fought in the Crimean War of 1854–6 at the Battle of the River Alma after which the Alma Tavern in Ipsley Street was named. He was awarded the Alma and Turkish medals and when he died on 9 November 1901, aged 76, it was said of him – '[he] was a British soldier to the backbone to the last'.

A Headless Cross man, Sergeant H. Porter, was a survivor of the Indian Mutiny of 1857–8, which was a widespread but unsuccessful rebellion against British rule by the Indian troops in the service of the British East India Company, which resulted in the abolition of the company in favour of direct rule of India by the British Government. Sergeant Porter lived on into old age and died on 2 November 1910.

The authors have tried to record details of the various conflicts as accurately as possible but as some of the events and images are over 100 years old – some even older – a little blurring of the full picture is inevitable. After all even newspaper reports and official sources often contradict one another.

We hope, however, that the wide spectrum of events in this book will give the new generation and newcomers to the town an idea of the conditions during the darker days of the past that Redditch, along with the rest of the country, has been forced to endure.

RIDGEWAY SKIRMISH

They came to muster
on the road to Worcester,
To Headleys Cross
on the Ridgeway track.

From Hewel they came
and Web Heath too.
A somber coated
motley crew.

With muskets primed,
and powder dry.
They waited for the dawn attack.

They were no test
for Cavaliers,
with plumed cockades
and sash to match.

They died in vain
for Cromwell's cause.
On History's page
A seconds pause.

R.J. Saunders

Early Days of the Worcestershire Yeomanry

FORMED in 1794, the first Yeomanry parade was in Worcester town centre on 25 October of that year. The troop was disbanded in 1827 but reformed on 29 April 1831 under the command of Other Archer Windsor, 6th Earl of Plymouth.

The Yeomanry were all volunteers drawn from the local gentry and farmers, and they were formed with the intention of putting down riots in industrial towns like Redditch where the struggle by workers to improve their pay and conditions often led to violence. It is worth mentioning here that the Windsors were landowners and much of Redditch belonged to the Hewell Estate.

In 1833 the 6th Earl of Plymouth died of apoplexy on his yacht at Deptford aged 44. A commemorative medal was struck and the Yeomanry erected a monument to his memory on the Lickey Hills, much of which the family also owned.

The 50mm diameter bronze medal designed by Edward Avern has the head of the Earl on one side in the style of a Roman Emperor and the Lickey Monument on the other side with the inscription – PLAUDENTE ET LUCENTE COMITAU – 'With the approbation and honour of his county'.

The foundation stone of the monument was laid on 6 May 1834 by Lord Lyttleton. It is a 91½ft high white granite obelisk on a 20ft square stepped base. In 1853 the Queen's Own Worcester Yeomanry Cavalry Regiment received new carbines which were kept at Hewell Grange and all the gunners came from the Hewell Estate. The gun detachment was disbanded in the 1870s.

The plaque on the Lickey Monument.

Medal commemorating the death of Other Archer Windsor, 6th Earl of Plymouth, in 1833. He was founder and Colonel in Chief of the Worcestershire Regiment of Yeomanry Cavalry in 1831.

The Worcestershire Yeomanry in camp at Hewell in the late spring of 1906.

Imperial Yeomanry shoulder badge.

More pictures of the Worcestershire Yeomanry in camp at Hewell.

The Boer War 1899–1902

REDDITCH did not greet their returning Yeoman and Volunteers with the enthusiasm accorded by most other Worcestershire towns. Indeed, only a few friends were present to congratulate Sergeants Laight and Kings of the 1st Volunteer Service Company, Worcester Regiment, when they arrived home on Monday 10 June 1901. Troopers Owen and Neasom of the Imperial Yeomanry had arrived home a few weeks earlier under similar circumstances.

However, this was soon to be rectified when at 6.30pm on Wednesday 19 June 1901, at the Royal Hotel in Market Place, the returned Yeoman and Volunteers from Redditch and District attended a dinner given in their honour, at which they were each presented with an illuminated address as reminders that their town's people appreciated their patriotism and gallant services.

The illuminated addresses, illustrated here, were the work of Mr F.T. Treadgold, an artist working from Salop Road. They were presented by Colonel Bartleet who commanded the 2nd Volunteer Battalion, Worcestershire Regiment, who made appropriate and complimentary remarks to the recipients. The presentations were followed by much cheering and singing. Trooper Neasom then responded with a few well chosen words for himself and Trooper Owen, as did Sergeant Laight for the Volunteers. There then followed a concert at 8.30pm to which all Volunteers in uniform were admitted free. The following is a list of the recipients who received an illuminated address at the presentation.

A soldier of the Worcestershire Imperial Yeomanry in a uniform of the Boer War period, c.1900. The photograph was taken at the Church Green West studio of photographer Harrison Speight who was there from 1899 to 1905.

Trooper Neasom was the uncle of local artist Norman Neasom whose illustrations of the World War Two bomb damage in Redditch appear later in this volume. The illustrated address presented to Frank Neasom is now in the Worcestershire Regiment Museum.

7316	Trooper F. Neasom	16th Company (Worcester) 5th Batt. Imp. Yeomanry
	Trooper W. Owen	16th Company (Worcester) 5th Batt. Imp. Yeomanry
6695	Sergeant C.V. Laight	1st Volunteer Service Company Worcester Regiment
6694	Sergeant I. Kings	1st Volunteer Service Company Worcester Regiment
6798	Private H. Tongue	1st Volunteer Service Company Worcester Regiment
6803	Private W.H. Woodward	1st Volunteer Service Company Worcester Regiment

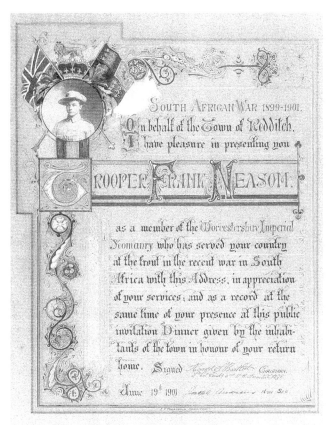

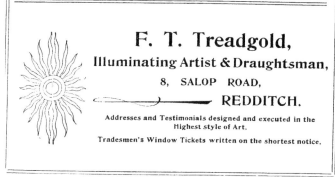

Advert from the 1906 Redditch Directory by F.T. Treadgold who designed and produced the 1901 illuminated address.

Trooper Frank Neasom's 'Worcester Jewel', a specially struck silver medal presented to all the Volunteers and Yeoman from the county who served in the Boer War of 1899 to 1902.

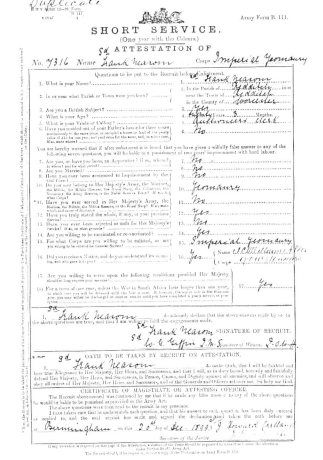

Trooper Frank Neasom of the Worcestershire Yeomanry volunteered on 20 December 1899 at the outbreak of the Boer War to serve with the Imperial Yeomanry in South Africa. While there he was in the 1st Contingent 16th Squadron (Worcestershire) 5th Regiment, Imperial Yeomanry and took part in actions at Rhenoster, Schwailyfontein and Frederickstad.

Tom Neasom and Charles White joined forces in about 1880 and Frank Neasom worked as an auctioneer's clerk in the resulting firm of Neasom & White. He was also a member of the Worcestershire Yeomanry.

Frank Neasom was born in Redditch in 1879, the son of Tom Neasom, auctioneer, of Church Green East.

Letter from Trooper Neasom published in the *Bromsgrove Messenger* in May 1900.

A soldier of Redditch Rifle Volunteer Corps which was formed about 1900. The photograph was taken in Lewis Brothers Alcester Street studio.

Letter from Trooper Neasom published in the *Bromsgrove Messenger* in July 1900.

Peaceful Manoeuvres

A very young looking sergeant in the Volunteer Battalion of the Worcesters. The photograph, dated August 1903, was taken by Redditch photographer Harry Edward Coles in his Victoria Studio at 91 Evesham Street.

A crowd gathered early one morning in 1907 in the approach to Redditch railway station to see the Artillery off to camp. Standing behind the dog is a boy named Joe – noted on the back of the card. In the distance is the Golden Cross Pub.

A photograph taken on 17 July 1909 at the Redditch Artillery Sports Day. The Easemore Road Barracks can be seen top right.

A crowd of spectators at a Military Tournament taken by Redditch photographer Albert Green on 24 August 1907, possibly at the Artillery grounds in Easemore Road.

The band of the No.4 Battery of the 1st Volunteer Battalion, Worcester Regiment, taken at Redditch in 1910.

Redditch Police Force, pre-World War One. Sergeant Best is on the extreme left.

1914 – The Rush to Volunteer

THE OUTBREAK of hostilities in August 1914 was followed in Redditch by a flood of local volunteers and many parades and processions took place around the town. Later in the year sustained efforts to recruit more men took the form of meetings around the district which were addressed by an assortment of military, political and local figures.

On 15 November a number of Seaforth Highlanders visited Redditch 'for recruiting purposes'. On 9 December a meeting at the Warwick Arms Hotel was addressed by Admiral Cummings. Recruiting meetings took place on 3 January 1915 in Studley and on 6 January in Redditch – addressed by Major Hall Edwards. On the 15 January it was Alcester's turn with MP Mr P.S. Foster addressing the meeting.

A Redditch meeting on 24 January was followed on 29 January by one at Headless Cross with speeches by Alfred Williams and Mr Sedden, and another on 11 February at Crabbs Cross. On 13 March there was a big rally in the town centre followed by the inevitable procession and a public meeting on Church Green.

However, the continual pressure for new recruits did not go entirely smoothly and at the Redditch Urban District Council meeting on 1 June a protest was raised against local recruiting methods.

The first flush of recruiting had already abated by this time and meetings were becoming less frequent – 23 October 1915 saw a meeting in the Temperance Hall presided over by Colonel Milward and an address delivered by Mr Eldred Hallas.

The rush to war and the constant recruiting depleted the town's workforce to such an extent that the issue reached Parliamentary level. On 24 February 1915, in the House of Commons, Mr Leverton Harris asked the Under-Secretary for War if he had received a request that Horace Gee of Astwood Bank, who had joined the Army, should be allowed to return home as he was required for the making of needles and parts for a machine that produced boots. Mr Tennant replied that 'the request could not be granted'.

A postcard showing Redditch Artillery marching through the town centre on 8 August 1914. The message on the back of the card reads – 'These are only some of the men, as they took the horses and guns to the station separately, 126 horses, 6 guns and 6 wagons, not so bad from a little place like this, is it? They had more recruits roll up than they could take, they had to send them to another Battery.'

YOUR KING AND COUNTRY NEED YOU !!

FROM the village home, from the city street,
  A stir is heard of marching feet,
And the clash of arms and the bugle's call
  Have thrilled our hearts and stirred us all.

Is it not great to have life to give
  For the glorious country in which we live?
Is it not great to shoulder the gun
  And to march where fighting needs to be done!
To march to the foreign despot's land
  Who has smeared the map with his bloody
                                     hand?

World War One patriotic picture postcard designed as an aid to recruiting. It shows Field Marshall Horatio Herbert Kitchener. He was killed in June 1916 while sailing to Russia on the HMS *Hampshire* which was sunk off the Orkney Isles.

Battery Sergeant Major C.R. Ellis, 21st Battery, Royal Field Artillery. 1871–1943. Cornelius Reuben Ellis, born in Colchester, joined the Royal Artillery in 1890 and served in India until 1899 when he was posted to South Africa to fight in the Boer War. Wounded in action, he was mentioned in dispatches three times and awarded the King's Medal and the South Africa Queen's Medal with Battle of Belfast, Defence of Ladysmith and other Clasps. He also gained the Long Service with Good Conduct Medal and is seen here wearing all three together with badges of rank as a Sergeant Major. At the end of the Boer War he came to live in Oakley Road, Redditch and joined the Redditch Battery, Royal Field Artillery, at the Artillery Barracks in Easemore Road.

A recruiting parade around the town on a wet August day in the first year of World War One, led by the Redditch Rifle Volunteer Band.

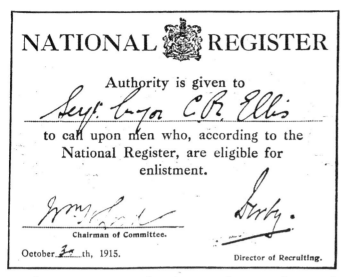

A card giving Sergeant Major Ellis authority to enlist men on the National Register.

A letter from Field Marshal Kitchener, presumably sent to all recruiting officers in 1915, urging them to greater efforts in the signing up of young men for the battlefield. One year later Kitchener himself was a casualty of the war.

WAR OFFICE,
July 1915.

Sir,

I wish to express to you personally, and to those who have helped you in your recruiting work, my best thanks for the energy that has been displayed by you all in the matter of Recruiting.

I would ask you to take an early opportunity of urging all able-bodied men in your neighbourhood to come forward and enlist, so that they may be trained as soldiers to take part in the War, and help to keep our forces in the Field at the maximum strength.

I shall be glad to hear of any reasons that may be given you by young and suitable men for not availing themselves of this opportunity to see service in the Field, where they are so much wanted.

I am,
Sir,
Your obedient Servant,

Kitchener

Sergeant Major Cornelius Ellis seen here at the Redditch Artillery Barracks, Easemore Road, in 1915 when he was a World War One Recruiting Sergeant.

Recruits on parade near the Barley Mow in Studley on 7 September 1914. Note the 'wounded soldier' in the foreground.

World War One recruits outside a local pub. In the window is a crumpled poster that says, 'Your Country Needs You.'

Lord Derby's Scheme and Conscription

BY 1915 THE Secretary of State for War required an army of 70 divisions which in practice meant that recruiting would need to be at the rate of 35,000 men per week. This was almost double the number of men that were volunteering so the coalition Government of the day was forced to accede to the demands of the military for conscription.

At the end of July 1915 the announcement was made that a National Register was to be compiled. It needed to be done quickly and a National Registration Act was rushed through Parliament which compelled local authorities to obtain the required information. All persons, male and female, aged 16 to 65, were obliged to register. They were required to give full details of their name, address, age, marital status, dependants, nationality, occupation and place of employment.

Anyone failing to comply with the requirements of the Act was liable to an initial fine of £5 with a penalty of £1 per day, every day, until the information was supplied. An estimated 23 million forms and explanatory leaflets, published by His Majesty's Stationery Office, were distributed and throughout the country 100,000 volunteers, mainly women, worked at amassing the data for the register.

On 5 October 1915 Prime Minister Herbert Asquith appointed Lord Derby as Director of Recruiting in a last attempt to see if sufficient recruits could be obtained voluntarily. However, the Derby scheme was doomed to failure as the Government knew full well that manpower on the scale required was not going to be forthcoming without coercion.

The Government issued a statement on 12 November 1915 that 'if recruiting figures are not met by 30 November then compulsory measures will be taken'. The Director of Recruiting's report issued on 4 January 1916 declared the scheme a failure even though approximately 2.3 million men nationwide had attested.

The Military Service Act, conscripting single men between the ages of 18 and 41, was put before Parliament in January 1916. In April the Act extended conscription to married men with immediate effect. Lord Derby had promised that no married man who attested would be called up until every single man had gone – this was proved false – conscription had become universal.

World War One Certificate of Attestation.

Recruiting in Redditch under Lord Derby's Scheme

LOCAL MEN who signed up were divided into almost 50 groups for the Parade around the town starting at 2pm on Sunday 9 January 1916. Groups 1 to 23 assembled in Easemore Road, the group leaders were officers, non-commissioned officers and men of the Worcestershire Volunteer Regiment.

Groups 24 to 46 formed up in Archer Road. In front of the Parade was the Redditch Rifle Volunteer Band and in front of Group 24 was the Redditch Town Band. The Redditch Boy Scouts formed the rear of the column. A number of 'Derby' recruits from Astwood Bank marched to Redditch to take part and were joined by men from Crabbs Cross and Headless Cross as they passed through. At 2.30pm the column marched around the town by way of Church Green West, Evesham Street, Ipsley Street, Alcester Street, Church Green East and Church Green West where the column halted by the church railings for a short religious service followed by the National Anthem, after which the men dispersed.

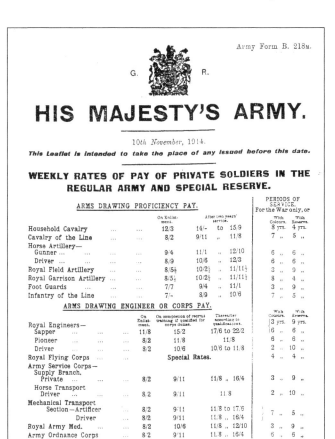

Weekly rates of Army pay in November 1914 for men on enlistment and after training. In only one instance does pay exceed £1 per week but 'increases considerably on promotion'. In 1955 National Servicemen were still only receiving 40d (equivalent to £1.40) per week for the first month of training.

The first group of men from Redditch and District recruited under Lord Derby's Scheme, form up behind one of three bands in Easemore Road at 2.00pm on Sunday 9 January 1916.

Local recruits attending the 15 minute prayer service held on Church Green at the end of the parade. The service was led by the vicar of St Stephen's, the Revd Cardross Grant MA; also present are Colonel H.S. Bartleet and Lieutenant Colonel C.F. Milward.

Redditch and the War.

The one outstanding feature during the first year of the Great European War, a feature that will long be remembered, was that the trade of the town and district continued exceptionally good. When hostilities suddenly broke out in August, 1914, considerable uncertainty prevailed in respect to business generally, and to the local industries in particular. Fortunately, only one part—fishing tackle—was seriously affected, and it is gratifying to record that this important local industry greatly improved towards the beginning of the autumn. A good share of war work was given to and undertaken in the town, with the result that the workers were kept fully employed.

The ladies of the town organised working parties immediately after the outbreak of war, and these continued their necessary labours, many useful articles being made and forwarded to the men on active service. The public appeals, including "Flag Days," were hailed as affording opportunities to assist the Allies in their unequalled task, and were liberally responded to, while the collection of eggs for the soldiers was an unqualified success. From private and semi-private sources there flowed a constant supply of gifts for the men in the trenches, for prisoners of war, and for the wounded soldiers.

The Club opened a year ago in Queen Street has been continued, and serves as a place for social intercourse of the wives of the sailors and soldiers.

The part played in recruiting and sending out of its sons in defence of the Empire and the smaller European States will remain a bright spot in the history of the town for many generations. The obtaining of recruits varied from week to week ; but the publication of Lord Derby's scheme gave a new impetus to recruiting, the published lists showing splendid results. Public meetings and demonstrations were held, these serving to keep before the public the urgency of the movement. The local Labour and Trades Organisation also issued a printed manifesto, which was freely distributed in the town and district. Two local men—Sergeant-Major Malins and Lance-Corporal Fox—were awarded the Distinguished Conduct Medal, the former also receiving the Military Cross of the Order of St. George.

The War Relief Fund continued to grow, not so rapidly as in the first months of the war, although the figures published week by week bespoke a regular source of income. At the end of November the fund had reached a total of £3,494 15s 9d. As a result of regular employment, the call upon the fund had not been heavy.

Owing in a great measure to the willing response of workers, the carrying through of the National Registration Act was undertaken and completed in a businesslike and satisfactory manner.

The effect of the operations of the Defence of the Realm Act was seen when further restrictions were issued in November regarding the sale of intoxicating drinks. These came into operation the fourth Monday in the month. Licensed premises were open from 11.30 a.m. until two p.m., while the hours in the evening were from 6.30 to 9.30. The Order also abolished treating in every form.

Extract from the 1916 edition of the *Redditch Needle District Almanac and Trades Directory* – it was not published in 1915.

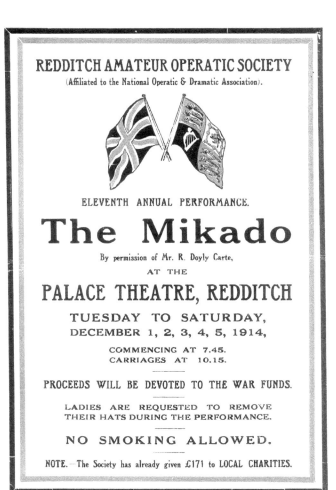

Redditch Operatic Society gave a performance of *The Mikado* at the Palace Theatre in December 1914 to raise money for the war effort.

Local Artillery and the Worcesters

THE FIRST enrolment of Redditch volunteers took place in 1806 under Captain Mence. The Redditch Rifle Volunteer Corps was formed on 28 March 1860; the officers were Captain R.S. Bartleet, Lieutenant W. Boulton and Ensign V. Milward, who were sworn in on 1 June. It is recorded that the Volunteers wore blackened brass buttons on their uniforms bearing a crowned, stringed bugle enclosing '39'. On a circlet round the rim were inscribed the words 'REDDITCH RIFLE VOLUNTEERS'.

The Volunteer Fire Brigade was formed in 1878 and incorporated an older Brigade. The Town Band was formed on 7 June 1880 from the previous Rifle Corps Band. The Volunteer Artillery Corps was formed c.1900 at the time of the Boer War. Another local volunteer uniform button (of which only one is known) was the 'LOYAL FECKENHAM VOLUNTEERS' an officers' button in silver bearing a crown over the letters L.F.V. It is thought to date from about 1805.

'H' Company, 2nd Volunteer Battalion Worcestershire Regiment was commanded, in 1901, by Captain C.F. Millward, with Lieutenant A.D. Bartleet. Both men were from prominent needle-making families. Their Chaplain was the Revd Canon Horace Newton of Holmwood, vicar of St Stephen's, Redditch.

The Company strength was 119 and their headquarters were in Ipsley Street. They practiced drill and held ambulance classes and used a firing range in Red Lane (Bromsgrove Road). This would almost certainly have been the one in Pitcher Oak Wood near Musketts Way.

By the start of World War One they had become 'H' Company, 8th Battalion Worcestershire Regiment, Territorial Force under Captain S.H. Clark with a Company strength of 89. The 1st Worcestershire, No.4 Battery, Volunteer Artillery Corps commanded by Captain W.S. Tunbridge started with a Drill Station in Birmingham Road. In 1901 the Lieutenants were H.R. Lloyd, B. Middle-

Several field guns of the Redditch Artillery assembling at the top of Easemore Road on 7 August 1914. The printing works of the *Redditch Indicator* are in the background.

No.2 Volunteer Battalion, Worcester Regiment, at Redditch Station. Off to camp in early August 1914.

A badge that was worn by many Redditch volunteers in World War One.

ditch and F.H. Evans, together with Surgeon Lieutenant Dr Morton and Instructor Sergeant-Major Fogg. By the start of World War One they had become the 2nd South Midland Brigade Royal Field Artillery, 3rd Worcestershire Battery – now under Major W.S. Tunbridge with a Company strength of 100 – and had moved to the Artillery Barracks in Easemore Road.

In December 1914 a new company – the Redditch and District Drill and Rifle Corps – was formed when the other Territorial Corps were sent on active service. Its Commandant was L.F. Lambert with Colonel C.F. Milward being described as its chairman.

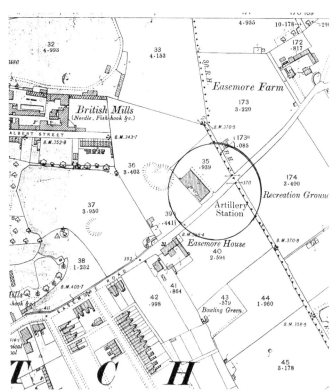

An 1880s map showing the location of the Redditch Artillery Barracks in Easemore Road. The building still exists having had many changes of ownership. At present it is the Redditch Community House and Gemini Dance Centre.

The Revd G.L. Michell MA who lived at 26 Beoley Road. He was the vicar of St George's from about 1910 to 1925. The message on the card reads: 'Your Vicar, trying to look his best at Chatham, 1917'.

A Gunnery Sergeant and field gun of the No.4 Battery, 1st Worcesters.

Men of the 1st Worcestershire, No.4 Battery, Volunteer Artillery Corps, at camp somewhere in Redditch prior to World War One.

Weekly orders for the local Volunteer Regiment were published in *Bosco's Budget* which was 'A weekly illustrated magazine of some things in general and of Bosco's pictures in particular' giving descriptions of the forthcoming films in the Public Hall, Church Road.

72 BOSCO'S BUDGET. 16th Oct. 1916.

3rd BATTALION WORCESTERSHIRE VOLUNTEER REGIMENT.
"A" (REDDITCH) COMPANY.

ORDERS FOR THE WEEK.

Sunday, Oct. 15.—Shooting, 11 a.m. Monday, Oct. 16.—Shooting, 7—7.30 p.m. Squad and Company Drill, 7.30 to 8.30. Wednesday, Oct. 18.—Shooting 7—7.30. Squad Drill 7.30—8. Physical Instructions 8—8.30. Thursday, October 19.—Promotion Instruction Class, 8—9, N.C.O. to attend.

Acting Orderly Officer for week, Sergeant A. Millward. Orderly Sergeant for week, Sergt. W. H. Wright.

F. J. Whiteley, Company Commander.

66 BOSCO'S BUDGET. 16th Oct. 1916.

THEY'RE DOING THEIR "BIT."

F. HARBON.

L. SMITH.

W. FOULKES.

A. P. GROOM,
formerly at King's Norton
Metal Works.

A. BROOKS,
formerly at Woodfield's.

A. CANTRILL.

A. SPENCER,
formerly at Enfield Cycle Co.

16th Oct 1916. BOSCO'S BUDGET. 67

W. HARBON,
formerly at B.S.A.

R. E. BAMBER,
1st Officer H.M.S. Franconia.
Recently torpedoed.

A. CANTRILL.

L. BIGGS.

N. E. BAMBER,
late at Bell's Music Warehouse

H. HARBON,
formerly B.S.A.

F. H. GREGORY,
late at Abel Morrall's.

We should feel obliged if our readers will kindly lend us Photograhs of their Relatives in uniform. Postcard size preferred. Please write on the back the name and former occupation as well as the name and address to which the Photographs should be returned. We are anxious to have a complete Picture Gallery of all Redditch men who have answered their country's call.

A Redditch soldier at camp on Salisbury Plain.

A 1917 postcard from France showing Redditch soldiers in front of a caterpillar tracked transporter for heavy field guns.

The band of the Worcester Regiment in World War One. Some of these bandsmen are from the Redditch area.

Redditch and the War.

The conditions prevailing in the town and district at the close of the second year of the great European war were in many respects similar to those at the end of August, 1915. Trade continued brisk, and those engaged in the staple and allied industries were fully occupied. The cost of living greatly increased and there were signs that the prices of the necessities of life would continue to advance.

It was anticipated there would be a heavy call upon the man-power of the country, and gradually but surely, many of the younger men of the town and neighbourhood were called to relinquish their prospects to train for and to assist in the defence of the nation and the empire. The parade of attested men in January was evidence of their readiness to serve their country. Week after week the Tribunals were occupied in dealing with the applications for exemption. Many who went forth to serve King and country made the great sacrifice.

On two occasions public warnings were given of the approach of Zeppelins, but, fortunately, the town and district was not visited by the "baby-killers."

The year witnessed numerous appeals on behalf of war funds. At Christmas a satisfactory response was made to the appeal for the Belgian children's fund, while the "flag days" were well supported. A liberal response was made to the fund of £2,000 for the "Star and Garter" Home for incurable sailors and soldiers, and in November the amount raised was £1,381.

The Alvechurch and Beoley district also raised £800 for the same institution. In addition to these calls, numerous semi-private efforts met with commendable response, and the sending of parcels to the men at the front was continued by private and semi-private organisations.

On August 4th—the second anniversary of the declaration of war— a largely-attended town's meeting held at mid-day on Church Green, carried the following resolution with enthusiasm : "That on this the second anniversary of the declaration of a righteous war, this meeting of the citizens of Redditch records its inflexible determination to continue to a victorious end the struggle in the maintenance of those ideals of liberty and justice which are the common and sacred cause of the Allies."

The lighting restrictions placed the town almost in darkness, a condition intensified by the early closing of many business houses. The order for all shops to close at eight o'clock every night excepting Saturday (nine o'clock) came into operation at the end of October.

The Redditch and District War Relief Fund amounted to £4,413 4s. 7d. in November, and the disbursements to that period were £1,240 17s.

Towards the close of the month of October labour unrest was in evidence in the town, particularly in the fishing tackle and needle industries. This was occasioned in part by the continued advance in the cost of living. At a conference early in November of the Needle and Fishing Tackle Employers' Association and the workers' representatives terms were amicably arranged respecting the wages of male workers ; no satisfactory arrangement, however, was concluded as to the wages of women workers.

Extract from the 1917 edition of the *Redditch Needle District Almanac and Trades Directory*.

Events at Home

World War One Identity Card issued by Feckenham Rural District Council in 1915.

From before the Boer War local photographic studios, of which there were several in Redditch, were kept busy taking portraits of a variety of service personnel as these few photographs illustrate. The girl in the peaked cap was wearing a Canadian Army uniform when she posed for L.L. Sealey at his studio at 16 Other Road. Also by Sealey is the picture of two soldiers, one in an Australian uniform, taken in August 1918 – their names are Ernest and Sam.

Beck's Boot & Shoe shop at 16 Alcester Street just prior to the outbreak of World War One.

The mixed group was by John Hensman whose Gainsborough Studio was at 5 Church Green East from the start of World War One to the 1930s. The single, bare-headed soldier was by Walter Terry who took over the Victoria Studio from Coles in 1904.

A postcard issued by local photographer Walter Terry showing early efforts to raise funds. The appeal is by Edward Prince of Wales (later Edward VIII). The card is postmarked 8 January 1915.

Adverts from the 1916 *Needle District Almanac and Trades Directory* made reference to the war but as far as possible it was 'business as usual'.

World War One school attendance certificate. Due to wartime shortages the usual morally uplifting story books were not available.

St. Stephen's Girls' School, Redditch.

OWING to the European War this Certificate is awarded to *Dorothy Ellens,* instead of a Prize for *Perfect Attendance 1915-16.*

J. M. Smallwood.
Class Mistress.

ALICE OAKTON,
Head Teacher.

During World War One rationing was introduced for certain foods, mainly meat. At this time there were many more people growing their own food and keeping livestock that at the start of World War Two when rationing was spread over a wider range of items.

School children were encouraged to 'do their bit' for the war effort by providing gifts for the Armed Forces on special occasions.

During World War One thousands of bicycles were produced for the Forces and Enfield motorcycles were supplied to the British, French, Belgian and Russian governments.

THOUSANDS of Royal Enfield Bicycles have been supplied to the British and Allied armies, which have nobly played their part in the great struggle. For all-round reliability and strength of construction in every part, combined with reasonable lightness and exceptionally easy-running qualities, the Royal Enfield Bicycle is incomparable. No Bicycle has better claims to your consideration in deciding upon a new machine, and none will more fully justify your good judgment. Ride a Royal Enfield and be sure of satisfaction.

Local Agent:—
A. BELL, Market Place.

THE ENFIELD CYCLE CO., LTD.,
Royal Enfield Works, REDDITCH.

World War One advert from the *Redditch Needle District Almanac and Trades Directory*.

During World War One the BSA Co. supplied the Army with large quantities of service rifles from its Birmingham factory. The BSA factory in Union Street, Redditch (originally the Eadie Manufacturing Co.) helped to fill the demand for large numbers of bicycles and motorcycles by the British and Allied Governments, as this 1917 photo of the factory interior shows. In 1928 BSA sold the factory and it became Britannia Batteries.

The World War One gas-powered Midland red bus seen here on Church Green is on its way from Astwood Bank to Birmingham and was one of the answers to wartime fuel shortages.

In the late Victorian and Edwardian periods crested china was a popular holiday souvenir. During World War One it took on a patriotic symbolism and the Redditch town crest on this plate is surrounded by the flags of the Allies. Note that Japan and Italy were Allies in World War One.

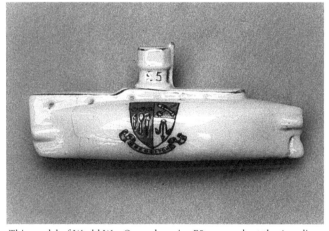

This model of World War One submarine E5 was made at the Arcadian China factory in Stoke on Trent. The factory also made models of tanks, field guns, aeroplanes, bombs, etc.

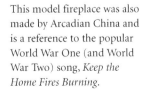

This model fireplace was also made by Arcadian China and is a reference to the popular World War One (and World War Two) song, *Keep the Home Fires Burning*.

'Tank Week'

Tanks were used in action for the first time on 15 September 1916 in the Battle of the Somme. 'Penny' postcards sold for sixpence to raise money during Tank Week.

The KAISER'S DREAM.

There's a story now current though strange it might seem,
Of the great Kaiser Bill and his wonderful dream.
Being tired of his allies he laid down in bed
And amongst other things he dreamt he was dead,
And in a fine coffin was lying-in-state.
With a guard of brave Belgians who mourned for his fate.
He wasn't long dead till he found to his cost,
That his soul like his soldiers had gone to be lost.
On leaving the earth to heaven he went straight,
And arriving up there gave a knock at the gate :
But " St. Peter " looked out and in a voice loud and clear
Said · begone " Kaiser Bill," we dont want you here.
Well, said the Kaiser, that's very uncivil—
I suppose after this I must go to the devil.
So he turned to his heels and off he did go,
At the top of his speed to the regions below.
But when he got there he was full of dismay,
Whilst waiting outside he heard Old Nick say
To his "Imps" now look here boys I give you a warning,
I'm expecting the Kaiser down here in the morning,
But don't let him in for to me its quite clear,
He's a very bad man, so we don't want him here :
If once he gets in there will be no end of quarrels,
In fact I'm afraid he'll corrupt our good morals.
O " Satan," dear friend, the Kaiser then cried,
Excuse me for listening while waiting outside.
If you don't let me in where can I go ?
Indeed, said the devil, I really don't know
Oh do let me in, I'm feeling quite cold,
Said the Kaiser, quite anxious to enter Nick's fold.
Let me sit in a corner, no matter how hot.
No, said the devil, most certainly not.
We don't admit people for riches or help,
There are sulphur and matches, make hell for yourself.
Then kicked " William " out and vanished in smoke,
And just at that moment the Kaiser awoke.
He jumped out of bed in a shivering sweat,
And said, well that dream I shall never forget.
That I won't go to heaven I know very well,
But its really too bad to be kicked out of Hell.

ONE PENNY.

Our Tanks & Gold will Win the War.

BRITISH TANK IN ACTION
SMASHING GERMAN DEFENCES.

VALENTINES SERIES
COPYRIGHT

PASSED BY PRESS BUREAU
FOR PUBLICATION 24TH NOV. 1916.

The tank 'Julian' being inspected by the local police force (Mr Franklin in peaked cap, extreme left) with the tank crew and a War Office official posing in front of it. The postcard is signed by the civilian official William Welby with the comment, 'Well done Redditch', and Wilf E. Davies, officer commanding the tank, declaring 'Am very proud of Redditch'.

"TANK" SUNDAY

APRIL - - 21st - - 1918.

TIME AND ORDER OF THE PROCESSION.

THE Tank will leave Redditch Goods Station at 3 p.m., proceeding by way of Park Road, Evesham Street, Church Green, to the Tank enclosure at the top of Church Road, in following order :—

1. Police
2. Redditch Town Band
3. "Tank" (escorted by Volunteers)
4. Urban District Council and Officers
5. Fire Brigades
6. St. John Ambulance Detachment
7. V.A.D.
8. B.S.A. Lorry with Guns and Shells
9. Boy Scouts
10. Discharged Soldiers and Sailors
11. Friendly Societies
12. "Tank" Committee and Workers
13. Police
14. Chief Marshalls: Messrs. W. E. Smith, and E. C. Patchett
15. Sergt. Major Ellis and Sergts. Wardell and Smith

ALL Members of the Procession are requested to assemble on the Footpath in Market Place, in the positions they will find marked out for them—not later than 2.30.

Public notice in the *Redditch Indicator* dated Saturday 20 April 1918 giving details of the arrival of the tank 'Julian' at the Railway Station for the start of Tank Week. It was put on display outside the old library in Church Road.

PUBLIC NOTICES.

Space kindly given by The Redditch Gas Company.

REDDITCH TANK WEEK.

WORKERS' DEMONSTRATION,

SATURDAY, 27th April, 1918.

All taking part in the Procession will assemble at Ipsley Green at 2.15 p.m. in the following order :—

Band.
B.S.A. Two Lorries mounted with Machine Guns and Shells.
V.A.D.
Fire Brigades.
Discharged Soldiers and Sailors
Henry Milward and Sons, Ltd.
J. English and Sons, Ltd.
James Blackford and Son.
Alfred Shrimpton and Sons, Ltd.

Arthur James.
Friendly Societies.
Herbert Terry and Sons, Ltd.
Redditch Indicator Co., Ltd.
Harris and Walford Ltd.
W. Woodfield and Sons.
S. Allcock and Co., Ltd.
Guillaume, Ltd.
Enfield Cycle Co., Ltd.
Abel Morrall, Ltd.

Marshalls—Messrs. EDWARD COX and J. B. GUEST.
Stewards—Messrs. PERRY, J. W. PERRY, PARKER, VINCENT and ROBERTS.

At 2.30 p.m. the Procession will proceed to the Tank by way of Ipsley Green, Alcester Street, Evesham Street, George Street, Ipsley Street, King's Arms, Other Road, Easemore Road, and Church Green.

A detachment of "A" Company 3rd Worcester V.R. and Boy Scouts will accompany the Procession.

On arrival at the Tank Addresses will be given by COUNCILLOR RAY JAMES, Messrs. A. GROOME, and E. BALL. Chairman—Mr. J. B. GUEST.

Details from the *Redditch Indicator* of the processions on Saturday 27 April 1918 when local factory workers, Fire Brigades, nurses, Boy Scouts and others would parade around the town led by a band, ending at the tank on Church Green.

The larger factories in the town sent their entire workforce to view the tank. Pictured here are workers from Herbert Terry & Sons spring making factory from Milsbro House, Ipsley Green.

The visit to the tank by workers from Astwood Bank needle-making firm of Joseph Perkins & Sons.

Tanks save Brave Lives and
Tanks cost money
—about £5,000 each

The more Tanks we have the more brave lives will be saved—the sooner will the fighters return to " Blighty " and you.

Buy £1,000 worth of National War Bonds and you will have provided one-fifth of the money necessary to purchase a Tank. If you have less than a £1,000—even if it is only £5 — you can still buy National War Bonds.

Then you may consider yourself the part owner of a Tank, and the British Government will pay you 5 per cent. interest on your money and a few years hence will repay it, with a premium added.

Your idle bank balance can be turned into fighting money if you will use it to

BUY NATIONAL WAR BONDS at the REDDITCH TANK

Details of the National War Bonds sold during Tank Week asking the people of Redditch to buy £1,000 worth of bonds. This would be an unrealistic figure even in today's affluent society.

These 'white collar' workers having their picture taken in front of the tank 'Julian' in April 1918 would appear to be from a firm of solicitors or something similar.

Buy War Bonds This Week.

Raleigh Bicycles next.

Space kindly given by The Raleigh Cycle Co., Ltd.

Agents—Alcester—E. Stanton, Swan Street. Redditch—A. L. Pitts, Evesham St.

Bank at the Tank

BUY NATIONAL WAR BONDS AND WAR SAVINGS CERTIFICATES—THE BEST INVESTMENT IN THE WORLD

This space is placed at the disposal of the Tank Committee by

Frank Walmsley, Tailor to Men of Taste **Unicorn Hill, Redditch.**

Don't worry about your Teeth this week.

Buy War Bonds at the Tank

and your Teeth at Vincent's next week.

Local firms' adverts in the *Indicator* reflected the spirit of Tank Week.

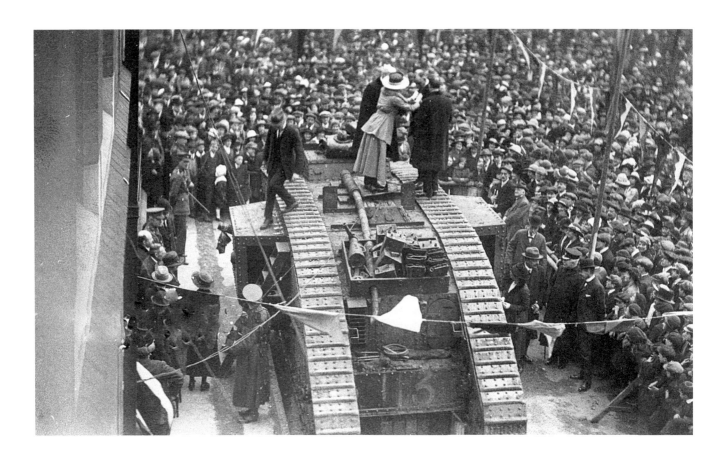

The townsfolk of Redditch turn out in force to view the tank outside the Institute (old Library) on Church Road.

YES! by all means, put every pound in the TANK you can spare—we must loan to the TANK, or lose to the Hun.

Mr. J. S. Murdoch, Men's Wear Specialist places this space at the disposal of the Tank Committee.

Redditch and the War.

The brief record of the third year of the war closed with a reference to the unrest prevailing in the Needle and Fishing Tackle industries. Happily, satisfactory terms were made and whatever danger presented itself in the form of a strike was averted. Generally, these industries —the staple trades of the town—continued to flourish, although greatly depleted by men joining the army, and many others taking up war work. During the year the labour organisations took steps to strengthen their position and several meetings for this purpose were held.

Without doubt, the year will be recalled as the time when much was done to increase food production. The local authorities gave full consideration to the matter. Government suggestions and requests were carried into effect. Land was broken up into allotments, and the workers of the town and district entered with zest into the cultivation of the same.

Food Control Committees were appointed throughout the district, and to these was given authority to fix the prices of various foods and other necessaries. Towards the end of October and early in November it was obvious there was a shortage in certain articles, and it was no unusual occurrence to see crowds of people waiting their chance of obtaining supplies.

Numerous appeals for war funds were made, with gratifying results. The "Star and Garter" Fund was completed. The sum aimed at— £2,000—was raised and local trustees appointed. The private and semi-private organisations continued their beneficent work on behalf of the Sailors and Soldiers and many hundreds of parcels were despatched to the various fronts. The Redditch War Relief Fund amounted to £4,823 14s. 6d. at the end of October, and the expenditure £1,280 1s. 3d.

"Baby Week" was observed, lectures and instruction being given. The week closed with a successful baby show held in the grounds of Stoneleigh, Mount Pleasant. National Service Week was also observed, and closed with public meetings at the picture houses.

Meetings in connection with the local War Savings Association were held, and the necessity of continuing this method of aiding the war was emphasised. At practically all the elementary schools in the district associations had been formed, the reports showing that these were rendering good service in collecting war savings.

As in preceding years of war, the call for man-power continued, and men left to join the forces, while the Tribunal dealt with many appeals. During the year the war claimed its toll of men, week after week bringing news of those killed in action. Several men from the district gained military honours.

No warning of the visit of Zeppelins was given, although it was known that a raider or raiders passed near to the town some time during the year. As on a similar previous occasion many people were alarmed. Fortunately, the raider passed over without doing any damage to life or property. The streets were still practically unlighted, and the tradesmen closed down an hour earlier than the recognised hour.

Extract from the 1918 edition of the *Redditch Needle District Almanac and Trades Directory*.

Casualties of the War

Tardebigge Village Hall was used as a Recovery Hospital for troops wounded in action during World War One. This group of soldiers and their nurses were photographed by Walter Terry of Redditch. The troops were entertained by Redditch Operatic Society on 6 March 1915. On 5 June 1915 a concert was given for them by the Redditch Madrigal and Male Voice Choir and on 7 August there was a wounded soldiers' fishing contest at Hewell lake.

Frank Saunders of Hunt End, Redditch who was killed in action in the first battle involving British tanks at the Somme on 15 September 1916.

Brass plaque inside Headless Cross Methodist Church commemorating the loss of Mr J.H. Harper (above) of 'Greenheys' Feckenham Road, Headless Cross, managing director of T.H. Harper & Sons, needle manufacturers, Phoenix Works, Redditch. He had been to the US on business and was returning on the SS *Lusitania* when it was torpedoed by a German submarine off Queenstown, Ireland, on 7 May 1915.

Several silver cigarette cases similar to the one illustrated are known to have been given to wounded soldiers who were at Tardebigge Recovery Hospital. The funding for these gifts probably came from the Earl of Plymouth who was at Hewell Grange just a few hundred yards away. This one was presented to Private Betterton of 6th Battalion, 8th Worcester Regiment, who was recovering from enteric (typhoid) fever.

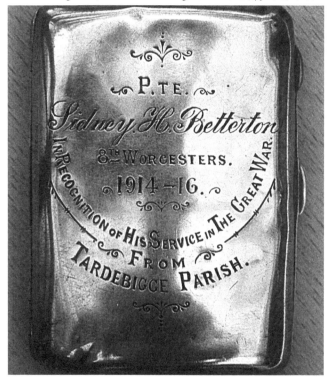

Smallwood Hospital Redditch, shown here in front and rear views, would have been a hive of activity treating the wounded of World War One.

Signaller Philip B. Jarvis, 289 Battery RGA. Killed in action in France on 27 October 1917.

A photograph taken in 1928 of the grave of Philip B. Jarvis of Archer Road, Redditch. The cemetery is near the village of Kemmel in West Flanders, Belgium, near the battlefield of Ypres.

CORRESPONDENCE.

Readers will understand that we do not necessarily share the views expressed by correspondents.

APPRECIATIVE.

Sir,—I have been out here nearly six months and, next to my letters from the dear home, I look forward with pleasure to the arrival of the "Indicator" which is forwarded to me regularly each week ; and although newspapers take rather longer to get here than letters, my patience is well rewarded, and, circumstances permitting, I am afforded a quiet hour's reading.

I say "quiet" as you will notice : but this is not always the case. Often, as soon as I have taken the wrapper from round my "Indicator" a kindly non-commissioned officer pops his familiar face in my dug-out and warns me for some urgent duty. Sometimes a line of communication breaks down, and such jobs as these must always be attended to without a moment's delay, or we hear the order "action!" given, and the boys then have to run to the guns. Again you see the shell rammed home, the lanyard pulled, and the shell sent off on its terrible errand. When we have a full battery of heavy artillery in action you may perhaps be able to guess how "quiet" we are for a time.

However, as soon as the guns cease and the din is over, and we are able to return once more to our dug-outs, then up comes the "Indicator." With keenest interest I read down its columns which tell me how dear old Redditch is getting along, even though so many miles away. After I have had a look at it my comrades usually have a glance through it.

The thanks of all of us out here are due to the Rev. Edgar Todd for giving the boys at the front a column of their own. I have read these articles with much interest and I am sure the time and trouble the reverend gentleman has given to these letters has not been in vain. I am sure that a clergyman's life is much taken up by his many exacting duties, yet I hope we may be favoured with many more of Mr. Todd's articles, which are so interesting, instructive and helpful.—Yours truly,

PHILIP B. JARVIS,
Signaller R.G.A.

British Expeditionary Force, Flanders,
September 8th, 1917.

F.C. Huins & Sedan Ltd. Advert from 1919 *Redditch Needle District Almanac and Trades Directory*. Signaller Philip Jarvis was one of five of their employees killed in action.

THE WAR.

SIGNALLER PHILIP JARVIS, REDDITCH, KILLED IN ACTION.

Mrs. Jarvis, 7, Archer Road, Redditch, has received official intimation that her son, Signaller Philip Jarvis, R.G.A., was killed in action in France on October 27th. This young soldier, who was 21 years of age, was a son of the late Mr. Walter Jarvis. He was well known in the town and held the affectionate regard of all who knew him. For some years before he enlisted he was in the employ of Messrs. F. C. Huins and Seden, Redditch. He attested under the Derby scheme and, although under exemption, his sense of duty was so keen and his patriotism so strong that he could not rest satisfied until he was with the colours. He "joined up" in September last year, and went out to France in March of this year. Much sympathy is felt for the bereaved widowed mother and relatives, who have received letters of condolence from the major in command of the Battery and from the chaplain. In a letter of sympathy to Mrs. Jarvis the deceased soldier's former employer, Mr. F. C. Huins, says how much "Philip was liked at the works. He was so unselfish at all times, so trustworthy and faithful. Although his life has been so short he has done much to make the world better. To myself he was as considerate and faithful as any son could possibly be, and he never complained, no matter how awkwardly matters went. Although he was under exemption from military service, he could not be persuaded to stay. His duty, he said, was to go and fight for his country. He was as cool when ordered to France as though he was just about to start on an ordinary holiday."

In Loving Memory of
PHILIP B. JARVIS
(Signaller), 289 Battery R.G.A., aged 21 years, who passed into the Higher Service October 27th. 1917. [a192]

The **Redditch Indicator,**
SATURDAY, APRIL 20th, 1918.

IN MEMORIAM.

DAFFIN.—In loving and affectionate remembrance of our dear son, PTE. H. T. DAFFIN, only son of H. and A. Daffin, of Cottages Farm, Ipsley, who died from wounds received in action in France, April 11th, 1918, aged 19 years. Thy will be done. Peace, perfect peace, with loved ones far away, in Jesu's keeping we are safe and they. Lovingly remembered by his dear Father, Mother and Sisters. [a115]

BAYLIS.—In loving memory of my dear son, PERCY, who was killed in action Easter Monday, April 9th, 1917. Sadly missed by Mother, Sisters and Brothers. [a134]

NEWBURY.—In proud and loving memory of GUNNER RALPH NEWBURY, R.F.A., who fell near Arras on April 22nd, 1917. "Into Thy hands, O Lord." Ever dear to Wife and little Son Peter. [a91]

MERRY.—In loving memory of my dear brother, PRIVATE SAM MERRY, 8711, 2nd Worcesters, who was drowned April 15th, 1917, on Transport Ship Cameronia. Lovingly remembered by his brother Fred, Sister-in-law and Neices, Aunts and Uncles. We little thought his time so short, In this world to remain. Or that when from his home he went, He would ne'er return again. We think of him in silence, No eyes may see us weep, But ever deep within our hearts, His memory we'll ever keep. A loving brother, true and kind, No better friend on earth we'll find. But God looked down, and thought it best. And took him home with Him to rest. [a89]

SOUTHAM.—In ever loving memory of our dear nephew, JONATHAN (NODDIE) SOUTHAM, who was killed in action (somewhere in France) March 31st, 1918, aged 27 years. "Until the day breaks and the shadows flee away." Lovingly remembered by Aunt Ethel, Uncle George, Emily, Lily and Ted. [a113]

DYDE.—Sacred to the memory of my loving husband, SERGT. C. DYDE (Studley), 5th Royal Berkshire Regiment, who, after three years' service in France, died on April 11th, 1918, from wounds received in action. A loving husband and a father dear, Beloved by his comrades, and a friend sincere, Nobly he did his duty, Bravely he fought and fell, And the sorrow of those that mourn him, None can ever tell.

ASTON.—In loving remembrance of PTE. HARRY ASTON, R.M.L.I., who died from effects of gas shell at 3rd Canadian Sationary Hospital, Doullens, France, on April 6th, 1918, aged 22. "Greater love hath no man than this, that a man lay down his life for his friends."—John, 15 c. 13 v. Lovingly remembered by Father, Mother, Brothers, Rosey and all. On the Resurrection morning, Soul and body meet again; No more sorrow, no more weeping, No more pain. [174]

ASHFIELD.—In loving memory of my dearly beloved husband, PTE. H. ASHFIELD, No. 457661, 3rd Worcestershire Regiment, who died from the effects of wounds in Military Hospital, Carlisle, April 8th, 1918, aged 26. Sleep on, dear Harry, thy labours are o'er, Thy willing hands will toil no more ; On earth there's rest, in heaven there's rest, We miss you most who loved you best. Sadly missed by his loving wife May ; also Father and Mother and Brother Frank on active service. [a88]

JOHNSON.—In loving memory of PTE. V. JOHNSON, 10th Lincoln Regiment, M.G.S., killed in action March 22nd, 1918, aged 26 years. We think we see his smiling face, As he bade his last good-bye, He left his home for ever. In a distant land to die. But the hardest part has yet to come, When other lads return, We shall miss among the returning crowd The face of our loving son and brother. Only those who have lost a loved one know the bitterness. Ever lovingly remembered by his Father, Brothers and Sisters ; also ever lovingly remembered by Flo. [a94]

ROSS.—In loving memory of LANCE-CORPL. JOHN THOMAS ROSS, eldest son of James and Ada Ross, died of wounds received in action in France March 26th, 1918, aged 21 years. A painful shock, a blow severe, To part with one we loved so dear. We little thought his time so short in this world to remain, Or that when from his home he went he would ne'er return again. We think of him in silence, no eyes may see us weep. But ever deep within our hearts his memory we'll keep. A loving son, so true and kind, No better friend on earth we'll find. But God looked down and thought it best. And took him home with Him to rest. Silently mourned by his sorrowing Mother, Father and Brother Jim. [a93]

Examples of losses suffered by the families of local soldiers, reported in the *Redditch Indicator* week by week for the duration of the war.

Indicator report on the death of Philip B. Jarvis.

Captain Philip Milward, who died on 7 December 1915 from wounds received in France. His family owned Washford Mills needle and fishing tackle factory on Ipsley Street.

The **Redditch Indicator,**
SATURDAY, DECEMBER 29th, 1917.

THE WAR

CRABBS CROSS SOLDIERS' DEATHS.

Official information has been received by Mrs. Lee, Crabbs Cross, notifying her of the death in action of her son, Pte. G. Lee, of the R.M.L.I., in France. The deceased soldier had been reported missing for some time, and was believed to have been killed. He had seen several months service in France. Prior to enlisting he was engaged at the Enfield Cycle Company, Redditch. He leaves a young widow and one child, with whom much sympathy is felt. He was a member of the Salvation Army Band, and a memorial service was held at the Barracks, Crabbs Cross. The deceased soldier has a brother in the Army.

Official news has been received by Mrs. Porthouse, Crabbs Cross, of the death of her son, Gunner Ernest Porthouse, of the R.F.A., in France, on November 29th. The deceased soldier was 21 years of age, and had seen several months' active service. Prior to enlisting he was engaged at the Royal Enfield Cycle Company, Redditch. He was a prominent member of St. Peter's congregation, taking a part in the conducting of the services. Three brothers of the deceased are serving with the colours, including Private H. Porthouse who, as reported in our columns, was severely wounded some time ago, and is now making favourable progress towards recovery. Much sympathy is felt with the mother, who is a widow, and has recently lost two daughters.

COTTRILL.—In loving memory of SERGT. CECIL COTTRILL, dearly loved son of Francis and Teresa Cottrill, killed in action December 3rd, 1917, aged 27 years. R.I.P. [a482]

THORNTON.—In loving memory of my dear husband, PRIVATE H. THORNTON, 31102, 4th Worcesters, who died in action in France, December 3rd, 1917, aged 33 years. A loving husband, true and kind, No better friend on earth can find ; For all of us he did his best, May God grant him eternal rest. We never knew the pain he bore, We did not see him die ; We only know he fell asleep, And never said good bye. Deeply mourned by his loving wife Phyllis and two children, Phyllis and Alfred. [a470]

The ribbon/memorial card text reads:

HE NOBLY DID HIS DUTY

In Ever Loving Memory of
my Dear Husband.

Private

James Ellins.

No. 32831,
3rd Royal Berkshire Regt.,

Was Reported Missing in France
April 20th to 25th, 1918,
and now presumed dead
July 17th, 1919.

Aged 30 Years.

The midnight stars shine on the grave
Of one whom we would have liked to
save;
For all of us he did his best,
May God grant him eternal rest.

Only those who have lost a loved one know
the bitterness of the word " Gone."

Always in the thoughts of His
Loving WIFE (Nell) and ALL.

253, Beoley Road,
Redditch.

An unusual type of card mounted photograph and ribbon recording the loss of Private James Ellins. These were produced by a Manchester company.

Redditch and the War.

During the fourth year of the world war the town and district manifested continued concern for its successful prosecution. Fortunately no unusual call for man power was made, the military claiming the " boys " on attaining the age of 18, and the Tribunal liberated those whom in its judgment could be spared from the several trades. The greater call was for money. It is highly gratifying to record that in this respect the town and district made a worthy response. The raising of money was the outstanding feature of the year.

The town had never undertaken a " lightning fund," but an appeal for a hut for the Y.M.C.A. could not be denied. Within a few weeks the sum of £2,739 13s. 6d. was raised for this purpose. This effort and result was the forerunner of bigger things. Tank week will take a first place amongst the efforts made for the war. During the night preceding the arrival of the Tank " Julian " there was a heavy fall of snow, much remaining on the ground on the Sunday. In spite of the unfavourable weather, crowds of people lined the thoroughfares, " Julian" and her crew receiving a hearty welcome. The weather the following day was ideal ; the snow had practiaclly gone. At the opening and subsequent ceremonies enthusiasm was at a high pitch. Speeches, concerts, and processions with bands, filled up the programme of a remarkable week. The proceeds totalled £350,567. No Tank had a more enthusiastic send off than " Julian," the streets being made impassable by the surging crowd of onlookers.

Later in the year the call was received that the Worcestershire Prisoners of War Fund required further generous and immediate help. The suggestion to organise the workers of the town and district for this purpose met with almost unanimous response. Redditch undertook to provide for all the men who had left the town. The manufacturers and workers contributed worthily to the fund, with the result that a good sum was guaranteed weekly.

The Tribunal was occupied week by week dealing with numerous cases, and the Food Control Committee continued its work. During the year a Lighting and Fuel Committee was set up, the duties connected with which were by no means of an easy character.

Early in the autumn a " Home Hut " was opened in Evesham Street for discharged sailors and soldiers and the men of H.M. Forces.

Studley and Mappleborough Green had gun weeks, and raised the splendid sum of between £40,000 and £50,000. The War Savings organisations in the town and district continued their necessary operations.

ARMISTICE CELEBRATIONS.

Close observers of the war detected in October a breaking up of the Central Powers, and late in that month Turkey and Austria, preceded by Bulgaria in September, sought for peace terms. Only a few days elapsed before Germany followed, seeking terms of armistice. The week-end—November 9-11—was one of subdued excitement and expectation throughout the country, and on the latter date at 5 a.m. the terms of the armistice were signed. Redditch heard the glad news a few minutes before eleven o'clock, when nearly the whole of the work-people broke with work until the morning of the 13th. Early in the afternoon a thanksgiving service was held on Church Green, preceded by a procession led by the Town Band. The remainder of the day was spent in orderly enjoyment. In the evening a large bonfire was lighted at the junction of Alcester Street and Market Place, and the Kaiser's effigy burned. Tuesday found the townspeople early astir. In the morning a big procession of school children took place, headed by the Town Band. After parading the streets, a concert was given on Church Green, popular vocalists and children rendering patriotic songs. Music (by the Metropolitan Works' Band, Birmingham) and dancing on Church Green occupied the afternoon. Early in the evening a monster procession was formed at the Council House, and proceeded to St. Stephen's Church, where the Town's Thanksgiving Service for the termination of hostilities was held. Those taking part in the service were the Revs. Leonard Bradley (vicar), Canon Newton, G. W. Clark (vicar of Beoley), B. Crosby (Wesleyan Methodist), H. G. Absalom and James Seden (United Methodist), J. Pearce (Primitive Methodist), and Mr. A. C. Millward (chairman of the Redditch Urban District Council). The Town and Salvation Army Bands gave their services during the festivities, and the officials of the Urban District Council assisted in making the arrangements. Telegrams of congratulation at the successful termination of hostilities were forwarded to the King and the Prime Minister, by the Chairman of the District Council.

Extract from the 1919 edition of the *Redditch Needle District Almanac and Trades Directory.*

World War One – The Beginning of the End for Bentley Manor

MARY MAUDE, the daughter of needle master Richard Hemming who owned Bentley Manor, Upper Bentley, was born there on 21 December 1853. She married wealthy Scottish landowner George Cheape of Wellfield, Fife. When he died in 1900 she became known to all as 'The Squire'. She bore him three daughters and three sons – by the end of the war only one son and one daughter remained alive and the Squire herself died in November 1919.

The Officers of the Worcestershire Yeomanry at the start of World War One. 'The Squire's' sons, Hugh and Leslie, are seated on the right of the front row.

Mary Maude Cheape, 'The Squire' of Bentley. A family photograph with pet Manx cat, Stumper and dogs, Foxie and Babs – taken by her daughter (also Maude) in 1899.

Her eldest son Colonel Hugh Annesley Cheape, born 15 November 1878, took the name Gray-Cheape on his marriage. In the Boer War he commanded the Worcester Squadron of the Imperial Yeomanry and he served as a Major with the Worcestershire Yeomanry in Egypt and Gallipoli, later becoming second-in-command of the 2nd Composite Yeomanry Regiment. He took command of the Warwickshire Yeomanry in December 1915. He fought in Palestine and on 8 November 1917 led one of the last cavalry charges by the British army at Huj, winning a great victory for which he was awarded a bar to his previously won DSO. He fought in Egypt until the Warwickshire Yeomanry left for France in 1918 on the *Leasows Castle* and was drowned when the boat was torpedoed shortly after leaving Alexandria.

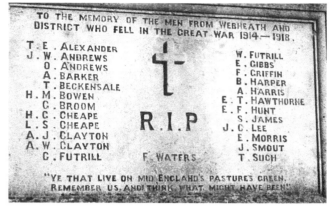

Stone tablet in the wall of St Philips Church, Webheath, recording two members of the Cheape family of Bentley Manor who did not return from duty in World War One.

A gift box bearing the motif of a hare and with compliments from 'The Squire' MH (Master of Hounds) Bentley Manor, Redditch. The badge is of the Worcestershire Regiment.

'The Squire's' youngest son, Leslie St Clair Cheape, born 5 October 1882, was a Captain in the 1st Dragoon Guards attached to the Worcestershire Yeomanry. The *Redditch Indicator* of 1 January 1916 reports of a telegram sent from the War Office to Bentley Manor with the news that Captain Leslie Cheape was wounded in action in Egypt – it was fortunately only a slight wound to the right arm. However, on Easter Sunday 1916 the Worcestershire Yeomanry was almost completely wiped out at Katia, Egypt, and Leslie was reported 'missing', later confirmed dead. In the same engagement his brother-in-law Lieutenant A.J. Cay also died. He married the 'Squire's' eldest daughter Catherine Beatrice 'Katie', who on 29 May 1914 had drowned in the sinking of the *Empress of Ireland* when it was rammed in the St Lawrence River. 'The Squire's' daughter Helen Margaret 'Daisy', born 15 May 1884, had previously drowned in 1896 in Loch Scridian, Isle of Mull.

George Ronald Hamilton Cheape, born 20 February 1880, was the only son to survive World War One and became a Brigadier General. He was awarded the Military Cross in 1915. He later commanded the 7th Black Watch in 1916 and the 14th Irish Rifles in 1917. He received the DSO in November 1917 and was at Passchendaele and Ypres in 1918. He also received the Croix de Guerre. 'The Squire's' youngest daughter, Maude Anne, born 14 July 1886, was the author of a book published in 1926 *The Squire of Bentley* – (Mrs Cheape) from which much of this information was obtained.

Peace

A humorous advert suggesting a peaceful use for redundant tanks.

Redditch and the War.

In last year's issue of this Year Book an account was given of the reception of the news that the Armistice was signed early in the morning of November 11th. By that act a heavy burden was taken from the national life. The spontaneous rejoicings exceeded those of Peace Day. On the terms of the Armistice becoming known it was obvious that the demands upon the several organisations called into operation by the war would in a short time not be required, and happily this proved to be so. The release and home-coming of many prisoners of war was the harbinger of a brighter day.

As many men who had suffered hardships as war prisoners were home in December, a suggestion was made to entertain them. This event took place on the Saturday afternoon and evening of January 11th, at the Palace Theatre and the Church Institute, Easemore Road. The Institute was tastefully decorated, and a warm and hearty welcome was given the prisoners of war.

The news that Germany had signed the Peace Terms did not interrupt business in the town. Generally the message was received as an ordinary piece of information, and the 28th day of June passed without local demonstrations of any kind. At Alcester on Peace Sunday a united service of thanksgiving was held in the Parish Church, and on the subsequent Sunday the Feckenham Rural District Council arranged and carried through a public thanksgiving service at St George and Matthias Church, Astwood Bank.

July 19th was Peace Celebration Day. The weather was not of the most propitious for the occasion. A joyful peal from the bells of the Parish Church conveyed the message of peace. Music by the bands was given in the Kiosk early in the day. This was followed by a civic procession, which was witnessed by densely packed crowds of people. During this part of the day's proceedings the sun made itself felt. After parading the main streets a meeting was held on Church Green West, when the chairman of the Urban District Council (Mr. F. J. Whiteley) voiced the feelings of thanksgiving that Peace had been made, and expressed deep gratitude to those who had served in many ways for the saving of the Motherland. "They humbly bowed their heads in memory of the men who had died, and they thought of them in pride and thanksgiving." The Vicar (the Rev. L. Bradley) read a Litany, and a portion of scripture was read by the Rev. H. E. R. Wassell (Baptist minister). The Peace Choir (under the direction of Mr. Alfred Hodges) then sang "The Homeland." After the service the choir took their position on a raised platform immediately in front of the West doors of St. Stephen's and to the pleasure of a great crowd of people gave an al fresco concert. Early in the afternoon was witnessed an attractive procession of the day school children, arranged and carried through by the staff of the several schools. They afterwards formed up on Church Green West, where they sang several songs appropriate to the occasion, and Mr. E. T. Moule gave a brief address. Late in the afternoon rain fell heavily, and continued for several hours. This necessitated the abandonment of the remainder of the day's programme. The Peace Choir repeated their music in the Church to an appreciative audience. Wednesday, the day selected for the completion of the festivities, was cold, but thousands of people crowded on to the Church Green where dancing took place, and later a display of fireworks was given.

Similar festivities took place at every village in the needle district. At the old town of Alcester the occasion was marked by the presentation of gold watches to heroes. Sports were provided, and the parishioners and school children were entertained to tea. Rain spoiled the evening's programme, but dances were held at the Corn Exchange and Town Hall.

The Redditch "Welcome Home" to returned men was a worthy one, made more so by the fact that the townspeople contributed £1,000 for the event. This took place on September 26th. The arrangements were carried through by a large committee. At one o'clock a peal was rung on the bells of St. Stephen's Church, and an hour later the procession started from the Artillery Barracks. As it proceeded through the several streets enthusiastic cheering greeted the men. The motto at the top of Easemore Road was "Welcome Home," while in other parts of the town mottoes with words of greeting and thanks were thrown across the streets. A civic reception was accorded the men. The chairman of the Urban District Council (Mr. F. J. Whiteley) gave a brief address of welcome and thanks, after the men had formed up on Church Green West. Dinner was provided at the Enfield Works (kindly lent), and sports were held in the grounds adjoining. A smoking concert was held in the evening, and as the gathering broke up the bells of St. Stephen's rang out a joyous peal.

Extract from the 1920 edition of the *Redditch Needle District Almanac and Trades Directory*.

Mount Street Peace Day celebrations, 19 July 1918, photographed by local photographer Joe Harman, of Lodge Road.

Peace celebrations outside Terry's factory in 1919. The man dressed as Charlie Chaplin is Chris Garner.

A scene from the 1919 Victory Parade outside Terry's office block. Note that the church next door still existed at this time. The front was later rebuilt as part of the factory and the main body of the church was retained and is still in situ today. The picture was taken by a professional photographer, Walter Terry, who was a member of the family.

Peace Day celebration at Lodge Road, 18 July 1918.

Procession outside Crabbs Cross School.

Cookhill produced this commemorative mug as part of their Peace Celebrations.

The Inter-War Period

The War Memorial outside St Stephen's Church on a postcard sent to America from Lodge Road on 13 August 1925.

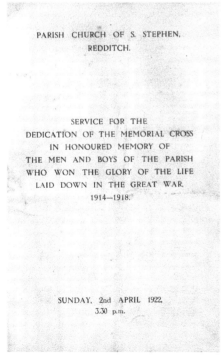

PARISH CHURCH OF S. STEPHEN,
REDDITCH.

SERVICE FOR THE
DEDICATION OF THE MEMORIAL CROSS
IN HONOURED MEMORY OF
THE MEN AND BOYS OF THE PARISH
WHO WON THE GLORY OF THE LIFE
LAID DOWN IN THE GREAT WAR.
1914—1918.

SUNDAY, 2nd APRIL 1922,
3.30 p.m.

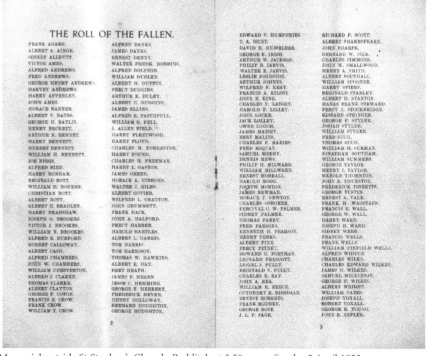

THE ROLL OF THE FALLEN.

FRANK ADAMS.
ALBERT A. AINGE.
SIDNEY ALLBUTT.
VICTOR AMES.
ALFRED ANDREWS.
FRED ANDREWS.
GEORGE HENRY ANDREWS.
HARVEY ANDREWS.
HARRY APPERLEY.
JOHN AMES.
HORACE BANNER.
ALBERT V. BATES.
GEORGE H. BAYLIS.
HENRY BECKETT.
ARTHUR N. BENNET.
HARRY BENNETT.
HUBERT BENNETT.
WILLIAM H. BENNETT.
JOE BIGGS.
ALFRED BIRD.
HARRY BONHAM.
REGINALD BOTT.
WILLIAM H. BOURNE.
CHRISTIAN BOTT.
ALBERT BOTT.
ALBERT H. BRADLEY.
HARRY BRADSHAW.
JOSEPH G. BROOKES.
VICTOR J. BROOKES.
WILLIAM T. BROOKES.
ALFRED E. BURFORD.
ROBERT CALLOWAY.
ALBERT CASH.
ALFRED CHAMBERS.
JOHN W. CHAMBERS.
WILLIAM CHESTERTON.
ALFRED J. CLARKE.
THOMAS CLARKE.
ALBERT CLAYTON.
GEORGE P. COTON.
FRANCIS E. CROW.
FRANK CROW.
WILLIAM T. CROW.

ALFRED DANKS.
JAMES DANKS.
ERNEST DENSY.
WALTER FREDK. DOBBINS.
ALFRED DOLPHIN.
WILLIAM DUDLEY.
ALBERT H. DUFFIN.
PERCY DUGGINS.
ARTHUR E. DULEY.
ALBERT H. DUGGINS.
JAMES ELLINS.
ALFRED E. FAITHFULL.
WILLIAM G. FELL.
J. ALLEN FIELD.
HARRY FLEETWOOD.
HARRY FLOYD.
CHARLES M. FORRESTER.
HARRY FOUND.
CHARLES H. FREEMAN.
HARRY L. GASTON.
JAMES GREEN.
HORACE A. GIBBONS.
WALTER J. GILES.
ALBERT GOVIER.
WILFRED L. GRATTON.
JOHN GRUMMETT.
FRANK HACK.
JOHN A. HALFORD.
PERCY HARBER.
HAROLD HARTLES.
ALBERT L. HARRIS.
TOM HARRIS.
TOM HARRISON.
THOMAS W. HAWKINS.
ALBERT E. HAY.
BERT HEATH.
JAMES F. HEARN.
JESSE C. HEMMING.
GEORGE F. HERBERT.
FREDERICK HEVEN.
HENRY HOLLOWAY.
BERNARD HOUGHTON.
GEORGE HOUGHTON.

EDWARD V. HUMPHRIES.
T. A. HUNT.
DAVID E. RUSSELDER.
GEORGE F. IRISH.
ARTHUR W. JACKSON.
PHILIP B. JARVIS.
WALTER E. JARVIS.
LESLIE JOHNSTON.
ARTHUR JOHNYS.
WILFRED F. KEAY.
FRANCIS A. KILSBY.
JOHN E. KING.
CHARLES V. LAIGHT.
HAROLD F. LILLEY.
JOHN LOCKE.
JACK LOLLEY.
OWEN LOUGH.
JAMES MAISEY.
BERT MALINS.
CHARLES F. MARIES.
FRED MCGAY.
SAMUEL MERRY.
DENNIS MEWS.
PHILIP H. MILWARD.
WILLIAM MILLWARD.
ERNEST MORRALL.
HAROLD MOGG.
JOSEPH MORTON.
JAMES NEWMAN.
HORACE T. NEWTON.
CHARLES OSBORNE.
PERCIVAL G. W. PALMER.
SIDNEY PALMER.
THOMAS PARRY.
FRED PARSONS.
KENNETH H. PEARSON.
HENRY PERKS.
ALBERT PINE.
PERCY PITNEY.
HOWARD G. PORTMAN.
LEONARD PRESCOTT.
LIONEL J. PULLY.
REGINALD V. PULLY.
CHARLES E. RAY.
JOHN A. REA.
WILLIAM H. REECE.
CUTHBERT E. RISSDALE.
ERNEST ROBERTS.
FRANK RODNEY.
GEORGE ROSE.
J. L. P. SAGE.

RICHARD P. SCOTT.
ALBERT SHAKESPEARE.
JOHN SHARPE.
BERNARD W. SILK.
CHARLES SIMMONS.
JOHN W. SMALLWOOD.
HENRY A. SMITH.
ALBERT SOUTHALL.
WILLIAM SPOONER.
HARRY SPIERS.
REGINALD STANLEY.
ALBERT D. STANTON.
HANAS FRANK STEWARD.
PERCY J. STOURBRIDGE.
EDWARD STRINGER.
GEORGE F. STYLER.
JOSIAH STYLER.
WILLIAM STYLER.
FRED SUCH.
THOMAS SUCH.
WILLIAM H. SURMAN.
JONATHAN SOUTHAM.
WILLIAM SUMMERS.
GEORGE TAYLOR.
HENRY J. TAYLOR.
HAROLD THORNTON.
JOHN R. THURSTON.
FREDERICK TIBBETTS.
GEORGE TUSTIN.
ERNEST A. VALE.
FRANK H. WAGSTAFF.
FRANCIS E. WALL.
GEORGE W. WALL.
HARRY WARD.
JOSEPH H. WARD.
SIDNEY WEBB.
FRANCIS WELLS.
FRANK WELLS.
WILLIAM PINFIELD WELLS.
ALFRED WIDDUX.
CHARLES WILKS.
CHARLES EDWARD WILKES.
JAMES H. WILKES.
SAMUEL WILKINSON.
GEORGE F. WILLIS.
ALBERT WRIGHT.
WILLIAM YATES.
JOSEPH YOXALL.
ROBERT YOXALL.
GEORGE E. YOUNG.
JOHN R. ZEPLER.

2

3

The Order of Service for the dedication of the War Memorial outside St Stephen's Church, Redditch at 3.30pm on Sunday 2 April 1922.

The service of dedication for the War Memorial outside St Stephen's Church, Redditch at 3.30pm on Sunday 2 April 1922. The Memorial was unveiled by Viscount Windsor and dedicated by the Archdeacon of Worcester.

The Service of Dedication of the Cenotaph in the Gardens of Remembrance in the 1920s.

The man on this card is John Gibson Blakey who had the contract to lay out the Gardens. He lived at 22 Bromsgrove Road, later at the Drive, Beaufort Street and was sometimes Head Gardener to the Revd Canon Horace Newton who lived at Holmwood. The gardens were officially opened on Sunday 16 July 1925.

The War Memorial in the Garden of Remembrance, Plymouth Road, as it looked in the 1920s.

The war memorial in St Luke's churchyard, Headless Cross. The picture was taken by local photographer, John R. Freeman, of Headless Cross in 1920.

REDDITCH URBAN DISTRICT.

REDDITCH CEMETERY is on the Plymouth road, opposite the War Memorial Gardens. It belongs to the Redditch Joint Burial Committee. It was begun in 1854, and now covers 12 acres. It contains 16 War Graves.

ASHFIELD, Pte. Harry Norman, 15686. 3rd Bn. Worcestershire Regt., transf. to (457661) 536th Agricultural Coy. Labour Corps. Died of wounds 9th April, 1918. Age 27. Son of Mr. and Mrs. William Ashfield, of Redditch; husband of Evelyn May Ashfield, of 2, Unicorn Hill, Redditch. YY. 14.

BARRATT, Pte. O. D., 4574. 4th Bn. Royal West Kent Regt. Died of phthisis 26th July, 1917. Age 35. Son of John W. and Ann Maria Barratt, of 230, Mount Pleasant, Redditch. CX. 6.

BROOKER, Serjt. G., 240547. Worcestershire Regt. 25th May, 1919. RR. 13.

HALFORD, Cpl. J. A., 3913. Worcestershire Regt. 13th Nov., 1915. Age 42. C. 10.

HAMILTON, Pte. William Reeve, 41489. 8th Bn. South Staffordshire Regt. Died of sickness 26th Sept., 1919. Age 40. Son of William Thomas and Clara Hamilton; husband of Olive Annie Elizabeth Turner, of 61, Evesham St., Redditch, Worcs. Born at Walworth, London. KK. 10.

HAY, Lce. Cpl. Albert Edward, 13503. 1st Bn. Worcestershire Regt. Died of wounds 29th July, 1916. Age 20. Son of William Hay, of 53, Hewell Rd., Redditch. HX. 18.

LAIGHT, Serjt. C. V., 2994. Worcestershire Regt., transf. to (507319) Labour Corps. 15th May, 1919. Age 57. DD. 12.

MARIES, Pte. C. F., 724. " H " Coy. 1st/8th Bn. Worcestershire Regt. Died of wounds 25th June, 1915. Age 24. D. 15.

PARSONS, Pte. Edwin, 3475. 5th Reserve Bn. Royal Warwickshire Regt. 6th Aug., 1915. Husband of Maud Eve Parsons.

PITTS, Serjt. H., 9429. 2nd Bn. Worcestershire Regt. 11th June, 1919. RR. 12.

PRESCOTT, Pte. W., 9647. Worcestershire Regt. 16th May, 1916. Age 52. Husband of Jane Prescott, of 5, Walford St., Redditch. A. 6.

RAY, Serjt. (Cadet) Charles Edward, 305024, M.M. 2nd/8th Bn. Royal Warwickshire Regt. 29th Oct., 1918. Age 29. Son of James Edward and Annie Elizabeth Ray, of 108, Oakley Rd., Redditch. NN. 9.

ROBINSON, Pte. J. T., PO/2363(S). R.M.L.I. 2nd R.M. Bn. R.N. Div. 1st April, 1918. Age 22. Son of George and Ruth Robinson, of Evesham Rd. Dag Tail, Crabb's Cross, Redditch. XX. 29.

STEWARD, Pte. Francis John, 19399. 13th Bn. Worcestershire Regt. 31st Jan., 1916. Age 19. Son of Agnes Bonham, of 32, Britten St., Redditch. A. 23.

STRINGER, Pte. Edward, 53199. 1st/5th Bn. Lancashire Fusiliers. Died of wounds 9th Nov., 1918. Age 18. Son of Edward and Elizabeth Stringer, of 4, Silver St., Redditch. VV. 16.

VALE, Pte. Charles Edward, 240760. 8th Bn. Worcestershire Regt. 15th April, 1917. Age 19. Son of John Sidney Vale, of 61, Prospect Rd., Redditch. CX. 22.

Extract from 'The War Graves of the British Empire' published by The Imperial War Museum Graves Commission 1931.

A float from the first ever Redditch Carnival in the late 1920s. It represented 'Old Bill in the Better Hole' referring to a popular World War One catchphrase.

The Redditch Salvation Army Guard Troop of Girl Guides in the 1920s.

A Company photograph taken in 1921 of 'C' Company, 8th Battalion, Worcestershire Regiment.

Redditch Police Force in the yard at the rear of the police station, Church Road, about 1930. Taken by local photographer John Hensman. Seated in the centre are Superintendent Frederick George Smith and Inspector T. Cook. The Sergeants are Harry Chancellor, Henry Loach, John Green and Ernest Price.

REDDITCH DIVISION.

F. Jeffery Esq. R.O.

" A Tableful of welcome makes scarce one dainty dish."
Comedy of Errors.

SIXTH

Annual Dinner

AT

The "Talbot" Hotel,
Redditch,

ON

Wednesday, Jan. 8th, 1930.

Chairman:
SUPERINTENDENT F. G. SMITH.

Chair to be taken at 6-30 p.m. prompt.

Secretary:
INSPECTOR T. COOK.

" Prepare for mirth, for mirth becomes a feast."
Pericles.

Folding wing aeroplane belonging to Mr Cave, a local businessman who flew from Beoley, on display outside Redditch Garage Ltd, Unicorn Hill, in the early 1930s.

The Redditch Division of the Worcestershire Police held their 1930 Annual Dinner at the Talbot Hotel in Evesham Street which was a popular venue for such events. Superintendent Smith and Inspector Cook were Chairman and Secretary respectively.

During World War One several bombing raids by Zeppelins took place over south-east England and the Midlands, with up to 13 airships taking part. One Zeppelin was shot down by Lieutenant W.L. Robinson of the Worcestershire Regiment and Royal Flying Corps, for which he was awarded the Victoria Cross. In 1931 a Zeppelin was seen in the skies above Ipsley Street and Ludlow Road, Redditch. The crew were probably taking aerial pictures of the town which would have been of use later in World War Two.

Graf Zeppelin over Redditch in 1931 taken from Ludlow Road.

Graf Zeppelin over Herbert Terry and Sons, Ipsley Street, 1931.

Graf Zeppelin over Milwards Washford Mill Factory, Ipsley Street.

'A State of War'

AT 11.15AM on Sunday 3 September 1939, Prime Minister Chamberlain broadcast the following message to the British nation:

'This morning the British Ambassador in Berlin handed the German Government a final note stating that unless we heard from them by eleven o'clock, that they were prepared at once to withdraw their troops from Poland, a state of war would exist between us. I have to tell you now that no such undertaking has been received and that consequently this country is at war with Germany.'

Three million school children were evacuated from towns and cities throughout the UK to rural areas in the first three days of September 1939. It was the biggest mass movement of people in British history. Redditch received children from Birmingham, the Black Country and Felixstowe in Suffolk.

These children were taken from their schools to the railway stations and bus depots in their home towns with little idea of where they were heading. Parents found out where their children were once they had arrived at their destination. Most of the children had not been away from home before and did not know when, or indeed if, they would see their families again. Some never did.

When, at first, the expected bombing of towns and cities did not happen, many evacuees went home, only to return 12 months later when the Battle of Britain and the Blitz began.

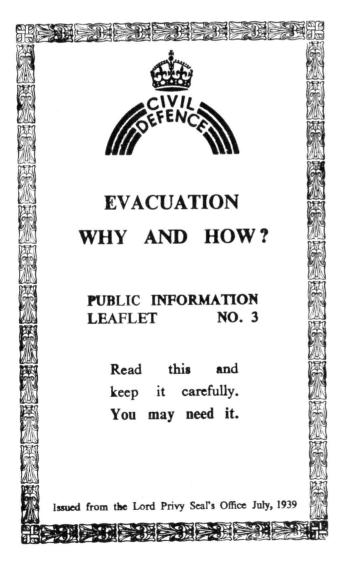

CIVIL DEFENCE

EVACUATION

WHY AND HOW?

PUBLIC INFORMATION LEAFLET NO. 3

Read this and keep it carefully. You may need it.

Issued from the Lord Privy Seal's Office July, 1939

In World War Two these premises on the corner of Ludlow Road and Mount Pleasant were the Army Recruiting Office with Sergeant Tommy Day in charge.

THE REDDITCH INDICATOR,

ISTRICT

MR. A. D. CHARLES.

SOCIATION WITH
NEEDLE INDUSTRY.

rs of Redditch needle in-
among those present at the
key Parish Church on
noon, of Mr. Andrew
s, of "Cotswold," Barnt
eath, on Thursday in last
rly recorded in our last
ne to pay a last tribute of
whose association with
industry extended over
century.

was a Birmingham man
he first became connected
ness life of the town 47
n he acquired the needle

BLACK-OUT TIMES.

	From*	To
Sat., Feb. 10th ...	5.32 p.m. ...	6.57 a.m.
Sun., Feb. 11th ...	5.34 ,, ...	6.55 ,,
Mon., Feb. 12th ...	5.36 ,, ...	6.54 ,,
Tues., Feb. 13th ...	5.38 ,, ...	6.52 ,,
Wed., Feb. 14th ...	5.40 ,, ...	6.50 ,,
Thurs., Feb. 15th ...	5.41 ,, ...	6.48 ,,
Fri., Feb. 16t.i ...	5.43 ,, ...	6.46 ,,

*The times in this column are also
the lighting-up times for cycles and
motor vehicles.

SUNDAY EVENING . MUSIC.

B B C. ARTISTES AT REDDITCH.

For the third of Ler series of popular
Sunday evening concerts, held in the
Palace Theatre on Sunday, Miss Mavis
Bennett brought to Redditch three
artistes of national repute and

CORRESPO

WHITE KERI
HOUSEH

Sir,—I suggest that
compulsory for eve
whiten the kerb out
the kerb of any ca
premises. A standa
arranged, and the it
be very little.

Many accidents an
caused through pe
an invisible kerb, a
nasty jolt when v
centre of the pavem
stepping off the k
entrance. The white
the dark and preven
would also be of g
foggy weather.

It would be a mo
those old lines :
" If everyone their
Devil's

Almost every week the *Indicator* reported prosecutions for contravening
the blackout regulations. Minor breaches resulted in an ARP Warden on
your doorstep yelling, 'Put that light out – put it out!'

HAIRBREADTH ESCAPE

Car headlights also had to be screened due to blackout regulations and
consequently road accidents became more frequent.

THE REDDITCH INDI

" CHILDREN FIRST."

TRANSFERRING THE
POPULATION IN TIME OF
WAR.

HOUSE TO HOUSE SURVEY AS
FIRST STEP.

A communication asking Local
Authorities to put in hand immediately
a survey of all accommodation suitable
for the reception of children and other
persons who might be removed from
dangerous areas in time of war, has
been sent out by the Minister of
Health, Mr. Walter Elliot.

It has not been sent to all Local Authorities in England and Wales, but to
those in which the dangers from air
attack are likely to be less serious and
which are therefore rsgarded as most
suitable for use as reception-areas for
the dispersal of some part of the
civilian community from the densely
populated centres. It has been sent also
to the Local Education Authorities for
these areas. In addition to a letter
from Mr. Elliott, outlining the principles
of the evacuation scheme, the Authorities have received a memorandum and
specimen forms for their practical
guidance in carrying out the survey,
and the text of a brief statement to be
left with householders, giving rates of
payment for the board and lodging of
evacuated persons. This survey will be
the first step in the Government's
scheme, the ultimate object of which
will be to perfect arrangements for the
" removal from the more dangerous to
the less dangerous areas of those whose
transfer is most desirable in the
national interest and on humanitarian
grounds."

Redditch Indicator report of 14 January 1939
about the early stages of the programme of
evacuation of children from areas liable to be
subjected to aerial bombardment.

As the German 'U' boats threatened to cut off
supplies of urgently needed raw materials all
possible existing sources were exploited. This
meant that salvage became a byword long before
the present trend for recycling. It also meant that
Redditch and most other towns lost iron railings
from church and park walls along with other
decorative wrought-ironwork.

REDDITCH RAILINGS FOR WAR MATERIAL

This appeal in the *Redditch Indicator* on Saturday 13 July 1940 was for spare aluminum cooking pots and pans to be melted down and used to build planes.

REDDITCH

Issued by the Ministry of Information ✠ *in co-operation with the War Office and the Ministry of Home Security.*

If the
INVADER
comes

WHAT TO DO — AND HOW TO DO IT

THE Germans threaten to invade Great Britain. If they do so they will be driven out by our Navy, our Army and our Air Force. Yet the ordinary men and women of the civilian population will also have their part to play. Hitler's invasions of Poland, Holland and Belgium were greatly helped by the fact that the civilian population was taken by surprise. They did not know what to do when the moment came. *You must not be taken by surprise.* This leaflet tells you what general line you should take. More detailed instructions will be given you when the danger comes nearer. Meanwhile, read these instructions carefully and be prepared to carry them out.

I

When Holland and Belgium were invaded, the civilian population fled from their homes. They crowded on the roads, in cars, in carts, on bicycles and on foot, and so helped the enemy by preventing their own armies from advancing against the invaders. You must not allow that to happen here. Your first rule, therefore, is :—

(1) IF THE GERMANS COME, BY PARACHUTE, AEROPLANE OR SHIP, YOU MUST REMAIN WHERE YOU ARE. THE ORDER IS "STAY PUT".

If the Commander in Chief decides that the place where you live must be evacuated, he will tell you when and how to leave. Until you receive such orders you must remain where you are. If you run away, you will be exposed to far greater danger because you will be machine-gunned from the air as were civilians in Holland and Belgium, and you will also block the roads by which our own armies will advance to turn the Germans out.

II

There is another method which the Germans adopt in their invasion. They make use of the civilian population in order to create confusion and panic. They spread false rumours and issue false instructions. In order to prevent this, you should obey the second rule, which is as follows :—

(2) DO NOT BELIEVE RUMOURS AND DO NOT SPREAD THEM. WHEN YOU RECEIVE AN ORDER, MAKE QUITE SURE THAT IT IS A TRUE ORDER AND NOT A FAKED ORDER. MOST OF YOU KNOW YOUR POLICEMEN AND YOUR A.R.P. WARDENS BY SIGHT, YOU CAN TRUST THEM. IF YOU KEEP YOUR HEADS, YOU CAN ALSO TELL WHETHER A MILITARY OFFICER IS REALLY BRITISH OR ONLY PRETENDING TO BE SO. IF IN DOUBT ASK THE POLICE-MAN OR THE A.R.P. WARDEN. USE YOUR COMMON SENSE.

III

The Army, the Air Force and the Local Defence Volunteers cannot be everywhere at once. The ordinary man and woman must be on the watch. If you see anything suspicious, do not rush round telling your neighbours all about it. Go at once to the nearest policeman, police-station, or military officer and tell them exactly what you saw. Train yourself to notice the exact time and place where you saw anything suspicious, and try to give exact information. Try to check your facts. The sort of report which a military or police officer wants from you is something like this :—

"At 5.30 p.m. to-night I saw twenty cyclists come into Little Squashborough from the direction of Great Mudtown. They carried some sort of automatic rifle or gun. I did not see anything like artillery. They were in grey uniforms."

Be calm, quick and exact. The third rule, therefore, is as follows :—

(3) KEEP WATCH. IF YOU SEE ANYTHING SUSPICIOUS, NOTE IT CAREFULLY AND GO AT ONCE TO THE NEAREST POLICE OFFICER OR STATION, OR TO THE NEAREST MILITARY OFFICER. DO NOT RUSH ABOUT SPREADING VAGUE RUMOURS. GO QUICKLY TO THE NEAR-EST AUTHORITY AND GIVE HIM THE FACTS.

IV

Remember that if parachutists come down near your home, they will not be feeling at all brave. They will not know where they are, they will have no food, they will not know where their companions are. They will want you to give them food, means of transport and maps. They will want you to tell them where they have landed, where their comrades are, and where our own soldiers are. The fourth rule, there-fore, is as follows :—

(4) DO NOT GIVE ANY GERMAN ANYTHING. DO NOT TELL HIM ANYTHING. HIDE YOUR FOOD AND YOUR BICYCLES. HIDE YOUR MAPS. SEE THAT THE ENEMY GETS NO PETROL. IF YOU HAVE A CAR OR MOTOR BICYCLE, PUT IT OUT OF ACTION WHEN NOT IN USE. IT IS NOT ENOUGH TO REMOVE THE IGNITION KEY; YOU MUST MAKE IT USELESS TO ANYONE EXCEPT YOURSELF.

IF YOU ARE A GARAGE PROPRIETOR, YOU MUST WORK OUT A PLAN TO PROTECT YOUR STOCK OF PETROL AND YOUR CUSTOMERS' CARS. REMEMBER THAT TRANSPORT AND PETROL WILL BE THE INVADER'S MAIN DIFFICULTIES. MAKE SURE THAT NO INVADER WILL BE ABLE TO GET HOLD OF YOUR CARS, PETROL, MAPS OR BICYCLES.

V

You may be asked by Army and Air Force officers to help in many ways. For instance, the time may come when you will receive orders to block roads or streets in order to prevent the enemy from advancing. Never block a road unless you are told which one you must block. Then you can help by felling trees, wiring them together or blocking the roads with cars. Here, therefore, is the fifth rule :—

(5) BE READY TO HELP THE MILITARY IN ANY WAY. BUT DO NOT BLOCK ROADS UNTIL ORDERED TO DO SO BY THE MILITARY OR L.D.V. AUTHORITIES.

VI

If you are in charge of a factory, store or other works, organise its defence at once. If you are a worker, make sure that you understand the system of defence that has been organised and know what part you have to play in it. Remember always that parachutists and fifth column men are powerless against any organised resistance. They can only succeed if they can create disorganisation. Make certain that no suspicious strangers enter your premises.

You must know in advance who is to take command, who is to be second in command, and how orders are to be transmitted. This chain of command must be built up and you will probably find that ex-officers or N.C.O.'s, who have been in emergencies before, are the best people to undertake such command. The sixth rule is therefore as follows :—

(6) IN FACTORIES AND SHOPS, ALL MANAGERS AND WORKMEN SHOULD ORGANISE SOME SYSTEM NOW BY WHICH A SUDDEN ATTACK CAN BE RESISTED.

VII

The six rules which you have now read give you a general idea of what to do in the event of invasion. More detailed instructions may, when the time comes, be given you by the Military and Police Authorities and by the Local Defence Volunteers; they will NOT be given over the wireless as that might convey information to the enemy. These instruc-tions must be obeyed at once.

Remember always that the best defence of Great Britain is the courage of her men and women. Here is your seventh rule :—

(7) THINK BEFORE YOU ACT. BUT THINK ALWAYS OF YOUR COUNTRY BEFORE YOU THINK OF YOURSELF.

(52194) Wt. / 14,300,000 6/40 Hw.

NATIONAL SERVICE (ARMED FORCES) ACT, 1939

MINISTRY OF LABOUR AND NATIONAL SERVICE.

Local Office, ...

WORCESTER

Date................................ 5 NOV '41

Mr. _O. F. Z....._

Heathfield Rd

Webheath, Redditch ...... Registration No. _R.H.D. 4629_

DEAR SIR,

I have to inform you that in accordance with the National Service (Armed Forces) Act you are required to submit yourself to medical examination by a medical board at

_10.15_ a.m. on _Mon_day, **10 NOV 1941** ....194......., at the p.m.

Medical Board Centre,

CONGREGATIONAL CHAPEL HALL

ANGEL PLACE.

WORCESTER

♦ If you wear glasses, you should bring them with you to the Medical Board.

On reporting for medical examination you should present this form and your Certificate of Registration (N.S. 2) to the clerk in charge of the waiting room.

A Travelling Warrant for your return journey is enclosed. Before starting your journey you must exchange the warrant for a ticket at the booking office named on the warrant. You should take special care of the return half of the ticket as in the event of loss you will be required to obtain a fresh ticket at normal fare at your own expense.

If you reside more than six miles from the Medical Board Centre and travel by omnibus or tram your fare will be paid at the Centre.

Any expenses or allowances which may become payable to you in accordance with the scale overleaf will be paid to you on application when you attend at the Medical Board Centre.

Immediately on receipt of this notice, you should inform your employer of the date and time at which you are required to attend for medical examination.

If you are called up you will receive a further notification giving you at least three days' notice. You should accordingly not voluntarily give up your employment because you are required to attend for medical examination.

Your attention is directed to the Notes printed on the back of this Notice.

Yours faithfully, C. R. COATES.

HAVE A DRIVING LICENCE BRING IT WITH YOU.

Manager.

[P.T.O.

6.

5—4885) Wt. 12690—4124 300 M 5/40 T.S. 677
0—4885) Wt. 15692—4175 750 M 5/40 T.S. 677

A call to submit to a medical check was usually followed by 'call up' papers.

DON'T CONTRAVENE BLACK-OUT REGULATIONS

Buy BLACK-OUT PAPER from your Newsagents

AMPLE SUPPLIES AVAILABLE.

To try and prevent enemy bombers identifying their targets and centres of population, the policy of 'the blackout' was enforced. After dark all windows had to be screened with heavy curtains and non-essential windows were papered over.

Civil Defence

ON 4 JUNE 1940 the then Prime Minister, Winston Churchill, broadcast the following speech to the nation:

'We shall go on to the end; we shall fight… on the seas and oceans; we shall fight with growing confidence and growing strength in the air; we shall defend our island whatever the cost may be. We shall fight on the beaches; we shall fight on the landing grounds; we shall fight in the fields and in the streets; we shall fight in the hills. We shall never surrender.'

Public Information Leaflet No.1. The first of several issued in July 1939 it gives details of air raid warning signals on sirens, hooters and police whistles. Also covered are the distribution of gas masks, lighting restrictions, fire precautions, evacuation, identity labels and food.

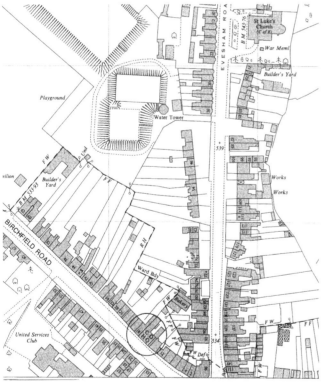

As late as the 1970s, before the end of the 'Cold War', air raid warning sirens from World War Two still existed and were maintained at strategic points around the town, on the tops of buildings such as the old Council House in Mount Pleasant, the British Aluminum factory in Studley Road and the Heath Spring and Notion Company, Birchfield Road. The outlying areas were not forgotten – in the event of Nuclear War the policeman at Beoley was provided with a portable siren which was operated by turning a handle. All this was controlled via a Civil Defence 'Ops Room' at the old Bristol Inn, 16 Birchfield Road (circled), now demolished and part of Headless Cross Green.

Pieces of hand-grenade, bullet cases, a badge and other items, found at the site of the firing range in Pitcher Oak Wood, Redditch. The site was used to train the Home Guard in World War Two.

A collection of pictures of No.4 Platoon, 'B' Company, 9th Worcestershire Home Guard. Redditch 1943 – CO Lieutenant Clarke.

A complete, unexploded hand-grenade.

This photograph shows 303 bullet cases from the Pitcher Oak range. The area has been used as a firing range since the early days of the Yeomanry, hence the name of the footpath through the wood – Musketts Way.

Members of No.4 Platoon, 'B' Company, 9th Worcestershire Home Guard, Redditch 1943. CO Lieutenant Clarke seated right. Others include F. Allwood and C. James, managers of Dixons Garage and Woolworths.

Part of a Home Guard soldier's kit – the knife is homemade.

'C' Company officers and NCOs, 9th Battalion Worcestershire Home Guard.

The Defence Medal awarded to all members of the Home Guard.

Badges and stripes worn by Redditch Home Guard.

Part of a Home Guard certificate giving details of the various training exercises and dates completed.

9th WORCS. BATTALION HOME GUARD.

C. COY. No. II PLATOON.

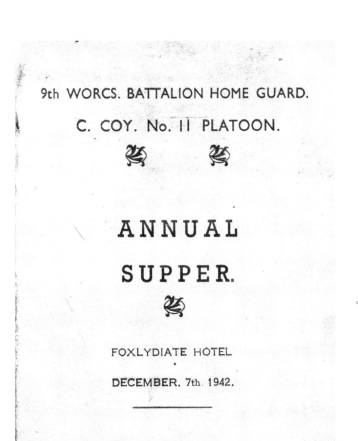

ANNUAL

SUPPER.

FOXLYDIATE HOTEL

DECEMBER. 7th. 1942.

"C" COY. HOME GUARD

COMPANY

DINNER

AT

TALBOT HOTEL
REDDITCH

OCTOBER 26th.

8-0 p.m.

TICKET 5/6

'C' Company Annual Dinner ticket, 1944.

A Worcestershire shoulder badge.

WAR EMERGENCY

INFORMATION AND INSTRUCTIONS

Read this leaflet carefully and make sure that you and all other responsible persons in your house understand its contents.

Pay no attention to rumours. Official news will be given in the papers and over the wireless.

Listen carefully to all broadcast instructions and be ready to note them down.

A badge worn by officers of the Worcestershires.

The War Emergency Information and Instructions leaflet gives a broad based list of instructions at the outbreak of war for the following:

Information and instructions via radio broadcasts.
The wearing of identity labels.
Air raid warning signals.
Lighting restrictions.
Fire precautions and dealing with incendiary bombs.
Closing of places of entertainment.
Instructions to drivers and cyclists.
Travelling by rail and road.
Telephone and telegrams.
Closing of schools.
Evacuation.
Food supplies.
Payment of pensions and allowances.
National Health Insurance.
General instructions.

The leaflet ends with the advice, 'Do not take too much notice of noise in an air raid. Much of it will be the noise of our own guns dealing with the raiders. Keep a good heart: we are going to win through.'

PUBLIC NOTICES.

REDDITCH URBAN DISTRICT COUNCIL.

AIR RAID PRECAUTIONS.

CASUALTY SERVICES.

VOLUNTEERS REQUIRED FOR

FIRST AID POSTS,
FIRST AID PARTIES,
WOMEN AMBULANCE DRIVERS.

Applicants will be required to attend the St. John Ambulance course of training and obtain the Certificate.

Form of enrolment to be obtained from :—

THE MEDICAL OFFICER OF HEALTH

Council House,
Redditch,
11th January, 1939.

Redditch Indicator ARP Notice, January 1939.

To distinguish a gas attack from an air raid, instead of (or as well as) sounding the sirens, the ARP wardens were issued with rattles to tell people to put on their gas masks. They were probably made locally to a standard design as the one illustrated has RCD 1945 (Redditch Civil Defence) stamped on it.

An ARP bell from Studley with the initials J.B. on the handle. Hand rattles were used to warn of a gas attack and hand bells signalled when there was no longer any danger from poison gas.

World War Two gas mask complete with its small can of 'Outfit Anti Dimming Mark 5' to smear on the eyepieces to prevent them steaming up when in use.

Children's 'Mickey Mouse' gas masks. When worn they gave off a rather unpleasant smell of rubber. When not worn they had to be carried everywhere in a cardboard box slung over the shoulder by string. During World War Two the girls operating the manual telephone exchange at the Royal Enfield office block were issued with gas masks that plugged into the switchboard and were equipped with a built-in telephone transmitter so that communications could be maintained during an attack.

To protect their babies during a gas attack mothers had to place the child's head and shoulders in the larger mask and tie tapes around its waist as a seal.

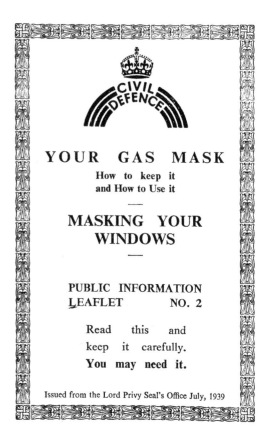

WORCESTERSHIRE COUNTY COUNCIL

REDDITCH URBAN DISTRICT COUNCIL

This is to Certify that

Miss R Dolphin

has completed a course of ANTI-GAS TRAINING held under the auspices of the Air Raid Precautions Committee of the Redditch Urban District Council, and has acquired sufficient know-ledge of ANTI-GAS MEASURES to act as *an Air Raid Warden*

Nature of Course attended *Modified Full Course.*

Name and qualification of Instructor *Rev. Edward White. C.A.G.I. 1764*

Date *24th February 1939.*

C. H. Bird,
Clerk of the County Council.

Chief Executive Officer.

This certificate does not qualify the holder to act as an instructor.

E9356

Prior to World War Two Redditch Urban District Council, through its Air Raid Precautions Committee, was preparing for gas attacks and air raids on the town as early as February 1939, as this certificate shows.

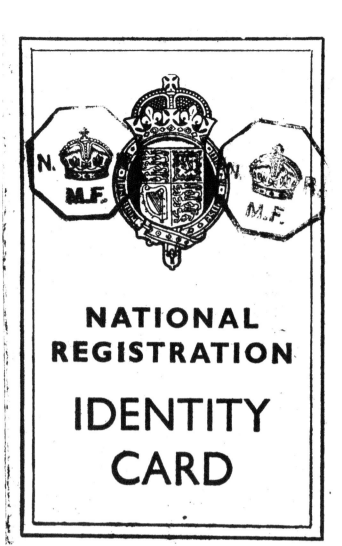

SHELTER PASS.

Name ....Mrs. O. ▓▓▓▓....

Pay No. .....1521.....

Section .Pointing. &...
          Cutting Off..

    is allocated to

....Canteen Basement..

SHELTER

· Carry this with you

ALWAYS

Don't forget
your gas-mask.

E.N.& F.T.Co. May 1940.

The English Needle & Fishing Tackle Company's Alcester Road factory also used the works canteen basement as an air raid shelter, as this pass from 1940 shows.

CENTRAL WORKS.

PASS No. **335**

Pay No. 1668. F. Name O. ▓▓▓▓

Occupation Finisher

Identity Card No. YJOT /149/2

Signature of
Issuing authority Basil King

Holder's Signature O. Hatton

During World War Two there was much made of the threat from saboteurs and 5th Columnists (spies) and everyone had to carry an identity card. Works passes were also a requirement – the one illustrated is from the Studley works of the English Needle & Fishing Tackle Company.

AIR RAID WARNING. YELLOW & GREEN FLASHING LIGHTS INDICATE THAT AIR RAID WARNING IS EXPECTED.

In a noisy factory environment, flashing lights were used instead of sirens for air raid warnings.

Air raid shelter direction sign.

Needle industry workers leaving the Studley factory and crossing the road to the air raid shelters. Judging by the happy expressions of the workers this was probably only a practice exercise.

The subject of this photograph is the opening of Crabbs Cross flower show but it clearly shows anti-blast walls built around the school.

Shrapnel from an anti-aircraft shell picked up in Beaufort Street on the morning of 12 December 1940, following the previous night's devastating raid on the town. Anti-aircraft guns could fire a 30lb shell up to a height of 35,000ft.

Along the Ridgeway, near Cookhill, these relics of World War Two still remain. The 'rolls' of concrete were PRB's – Portable Road Blocks, which would have been moved into place with an iron bar down the central hole so that they could be rolled into the required position.

Redditch Company Home Guard, 1943.

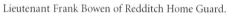

Lieutenant Frank Bowen of Redditch Home Guard.

A Home Guard troop on a training exercise in the lanes near Beoley.

An Allen family photograph. In the background can be seen the air raid shelter that stood on what is now the car park of the Abbey Stadium, Birmingham Road.

A World War Two water tank on Milwards premises at the corner of Other Road which would have been used by the Auxiliary Fire Service in the event of air raids. In the 1960s, Milwards used it for fly casting lessons given by Terry Thomas, a local television fishing personality.

Maurice Clarke. Auxiliary Fire Service, Redditch, 1941.

A fire engine outside Sandiland's Station Café, Station Approach. This type of engine was used by the Fire Brigade at Red Lion Street. Auxiliary Fire Service and National Fire Service personnel manned various substations such as Easemore Road Drill Hall. The Lamb and Flag, Unicorn Hill, was used as a mess room and sleeping quarters, with the equipment stored at Redditch Garages at the bottom of the hill. The Auxiliary Fire Service used trailer pumps towed behind a commandeered limousine capable of holding the crew of four to six men.

Fire Service discharge certificate issued at the end of World War Two.

NATIONAL FIRE SERVICE

CERTIFICATE OF SERVICE

Name (in full) .... Maurice Henry Clarke ....

National Fire Service No. ... 597247 ...... Date of discharge 31.8.45 ....

Rank on discharge Fireman ....

Cause of discharge Reduction of Establishment on Cessation of Hostilities ....

	WITH LOCAL AUTHORITY FIRE BRIGADE	WITH NATIONAL FIRE SERVICE
WHOLE-TIME SERVICE	from	from
	to	to
PART-TIME SERVICE	from 13.1.41.	from 18.8.41.
	to 17.8.41.	to 31.8.45.

31st August, ... 19 45. .... Fire Force Commander.

Local MP, Sir John Wardlaw-Milne, congratulating lady members of the English Needle and Fishing Tackle firewatchers who had just passed their stirrup-pump test.

5191

WORCESTERSHIRE CONSTABULARY.

*T*HIS IS TO CERTIFY that the Bearer

N. BREARLEY
....

is a Member of the

WORCESTERSHIRE DEFENCE VOLUNTEERS.

Colonel.
County Sub-Area Commander.

Needle Industries Fire Brigade outside Central Works Canteen, Studley, in November 1944.

Crabbs Cross, World War Two ARP wardens. Some names are: Back row, W. Brown (2nd from left), A. Hale (3rd from right) and John Smith. Front row, John Bird (4th from right), Mrs Groves, Mr and Mrs Molesworth and daughter, Miss Hilda Portman.

Redditch District Special Constabulary. Photographed at the end of World War Two at the rear of the police station which was then in Church Road, Redditch.

Redditch Special Constables being inspected by the Chief Constable in 1943.

Royal Enfield Cycle Company Home Guard.

Royal Enfield Home Guard football team. Back row: Jimmy Grant, Bert Aymes, Norman 'Noddy' Ralph, Harry Aston, Backet Court. Middle row: Cliff Lewis, George Kearsley, Lambert Roberts. Front row: 'Dinky' Griffin, Pearson, Jack Aymes, Oliver Wythes, Bill Holder, Alan Smith, Eric Tillesley.

Crabbs Cross Home Guard.

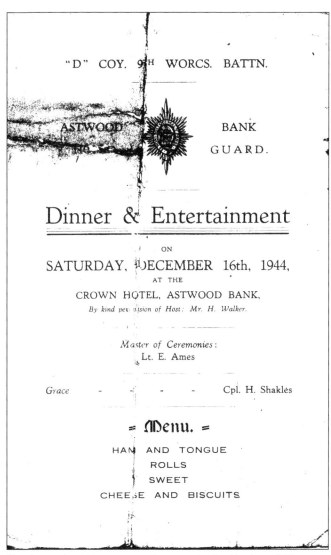

"D" COY. 9TH WORCS. BATTN.

ASTWOOD BANK GUARD.

Dinner & Entertainment

ON

SATURDAY, DECEMBER 16th, 1944,

AT THE

CROWN HOTEL, ASTWOOD BANK,

By kind permission of Host: Mr. H. Walker.

Master of Ceremonies:
Lt. E. Ames

Grace - - - - Cpl. H. Shakles

= Menu. =

HAM AND TONGUE
ROLLS
SWEET
CHEESE AND BISCUITS

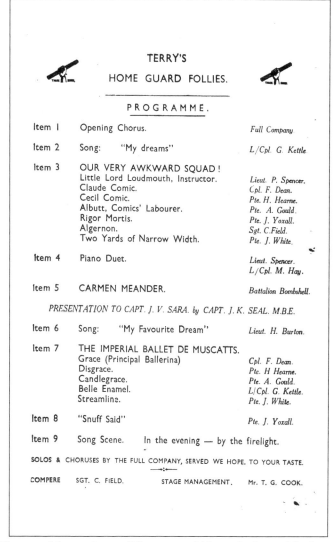

TERRY'S HOME GUARD FOLLIES.

PROGRAMME.

Item 1	Opening Chorus.	*Full Company.*
Item 2	Song: "My dreams"	*L/Cpl. G. Kettle.*
Item 3	OUR VERY AWKWARD SQUAD !	
	Little Lord Loudmouth, Instructor.	*Lieut. P. Spencer.*
	Claude Comic.	*Cpl. F. Dean.*
	Cecil Comic.	*Pte. H. Hearne.*
	Albutt, Comics' Labourer.	*Pte. A. Gould.*
	Rigor Mortis.	*Pte. J. Yoxall.*
	Algernon.	*Sgt. C. Field.*
	Two Yards of Narrow Width.	*Pte. J. White.*
Item 4	Piano Duet.	*Lieut. Spencer.*
		L/Cpl. M. Hay.
Item 5	CARMEN MEANDER.	*Battalion Bombshell.*

PRESENTATION TO CAPT. J. V. SARA. by CAPT. J. K. SEAL. M.B.E.

Item 6	Song: "My Favourite Dream"	*Lieut. H. Burton.*
Item 7	THE IMPERIAL BALLET DE MUSCATTS.	
	Grace (Principal Ballerina)	*Cpl. F. Dean.*
	Disgrace.	*Pte. H Hearne.*
	Candlegrace.	*Pte. A. Gould.*
	Belle Enamel.	*L/Cpl. G. Kettle.*
	Streamline.	*Pte. J. White.*
Item 8	"Snuff Said"	*Pte. J. Yoxall.*
Item 9	Song Scene. In the evening — by the firelight.	

SOLOS & CHORUSES BY THE FULL COMPANY, SERVED WE HOPE, TO YOUR TASTE.

COMPERE SGT. C. FIELD. STAGE MANAGEMENT. Mr. T. G. COOK.

Despite wartime shortages, morale was maintained by Annual Dinners and 'homemade' entertainment. 'D' company, which was the Astwood Bank Home Guard, enjoyed a simple meal of ham and tongue rolls, a sweet and cheese and biscuits at the Crown in December 1944. Herbert Terry & Sons Home Guard Follies could put on a complete revue.

A group of Red Cross nurses on the lawn of the Dorothy Terry Red Cross house in Headless Cross. Not many of the names are known. Back row, 3rd from right, Margaret James. Middle row, left to right, Mrs Hins, Phyllis Dixon, unknown, unknown, unknown, Estelle Thorne, unknown, unknown, Enid Davies, Madge James, unknown, unknown, unknown, unknown, unknown. Front row, left to right, Helen Taylor, Ms Johnston, Mrs Thompson, Blanche Hughes, unknown, Mr Dine (Colonel in Chief), Mrs Houghton, Dr Potts, unknown, unknown, Mrs Buffey, Mrs Jarvis, unknown.

WAR ORGANISATION
OF THE
BRITISH RED CROSS SOCIETY
AND
ORDER OF ST JOHN OF JERUSALEM

Presented to

Geoffrey Allen

Redditch Ambulance Division

in recognition of devoted service to
the cause of humanity
during the second world war

1939~1945

George R.I.

Sovereign Head.
Order of St. John of Jerusalem.

Elizabeth R

President.
British Red Cross Society.

It is impossible to over emphasise the debt of gratitude owed to the Red Cross for their efforts in World War Two, such as nursing, getting food parcels to prisoners of war and much more.

Civil Defence ambulance drivers, VAD nursing assistants and Smallwood Hospital nurses at the rear of the Hospital by the Mortuary and old Physiotherapy Department. Standing left to right, Enid Davie, unknown, Doug Turner, Mr Watts, unknown, Mr Finch, Odette Bennett. Seated left to right, unknown, Sheila Styler, unknown, Beryl Steel, unknown.

Rationing

FOOD and clothing was rationed for most of World War Two and even several years after. Ration books were issued to each family to ensure fair distribution of available resources. The books held coupons for the various items and they were removed by the retailer whose name was stamped in the book and with whom you were registered. Even if you had coupons for sweets, for example, very often they were not available in the shops. Under these conditions it is not surprising that people turned to the 'black market' for items that were unavailable elsewhere.

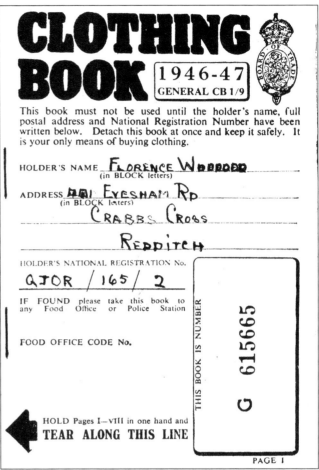

A post-war ration book for clothing.

REASONS FOR RATIONING

War has meant the re-planning of our food supplies. Half our meat and most of our bacon, butter and sugar come from overseas. Here are four reasons for rationing :—

1 RATIONING PREVENTS WASTE OF FOOD We must not ask our sailors to bring us unnecessary food cargoes at the risk of their lives.

2 RATIONING INCREASES OUR WAR EFFORT Our shipping carries food, and armaments in their raw and finished state, and other essential raw materials for home consumption and the export trade. To reduce our purchases of food abroad is to release ships for bringing us other imports. So we shall strengthen our war effort.

3 RATIONING DIVIDES SUPPLIES EQUALLY There will be ample supplies for our 44½ million people, but we must divide them fairly, everyone being treated alike. No one must be left out.

4 RATIONING PREVENTS UNCERTAINTY Your Ration Book assures you of your fair share. Rationing means that there will be no uncertainty — and no queues.

YOUR RATION BOOK IS YOUR PASSPORT TO EASY PURCHASING OF BACON & HAM, BUTTER AND SUGAR

Public Notice in the *Redditch Indicator* on Saturday 13 January 1940.

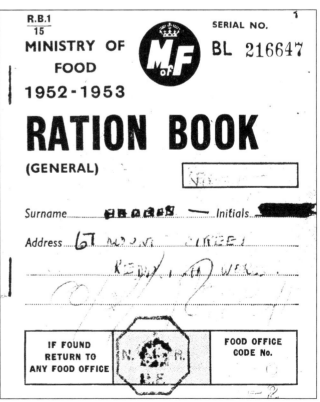

A post-war ration book for general food items.

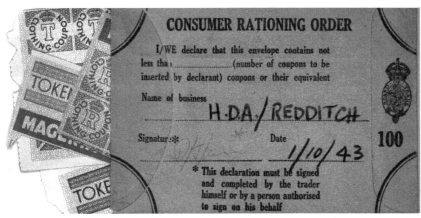

The company provided High Duty Alloys workforce with protective overalls which were still subject to rationing, though they were given an extra allocation of coupons.

Public Notice in the *Redditch Indicator* on Saturday 6 January 1940.

Families had to register with one retailer for each kind of food and coupons were cancelled or cut out as the allocation was used up.

WASTE THE FOOD AND HELP THE HUN

A British poster designed to prevent food wastage as all imported goods coming in by boat were open to attack by German 'U' boats. A 'Dig for Victory' campaign was launched and in every street there appeared a 'Pig Bin' to take any wastage.

The wartime 'Pig Bin'.

Another World War Two poster on the theme of waste.

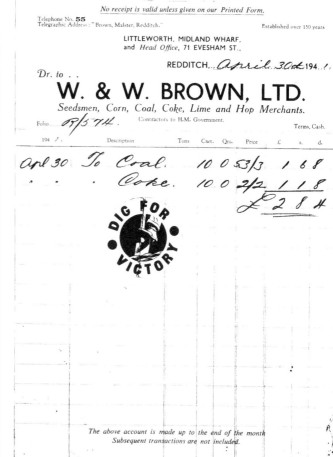

A 1941 bill for coal and coke from Brown's of Evesham Street with a 'Dig for Victory' sticker attached.

From the *Redditch Indicator* of 1 June 1940. A patriotic advert by the brewing industry extolling the virtues of paying more tax and drinking more beer.

World War Two saw many restrictions on travel in an attempt to preserve fuel supplies for essential services. Petrol for official use was dyed red to prevent 'siphoning off' for private use.

POUNDS
from
PENNIES

When you order a pint of beer nowadays, several important things happen. You do yourself good — because of the wholesome barley-malt and hops in it. You become a more cheering and cheerful citizen of the country.

And you contribute a new, 1940, *extra* penny to the Government.

One penny does not seem much, but the *total* tax on a pint of beer means a lot. Count up the duty paid by all the British men and women who like an occasional glass of beer — in industrial towns, in big cities, in country villages, in lonely inns on the moors or by some sea-shore — and what does it amount to in pounds?

Per year — estimated at over one hundred million pounds.

For the nation, as for the citizen, beer is indeed best. For your *own* good — as well as the nation's good — stick to beer!

Events

War Weapons Week
11–18 January 1941

An announcement in the *Redditch Indicator* on Saturday 11 January 1941 of the forthcoming Civil Defence Parade around the town to encourage people to buy more War Bonds, Defence Bonds and Saving Certificates.

The War Weapons Week Civil Defence Parade around Redditch town centre on Saturday 18 January 1941 moved off at 2.30pm and consisted of every possible unit available, including the Boy Scouts and Girl Guides.

The Home Guard on parade in Church Green West at the end of War Weapons Week.

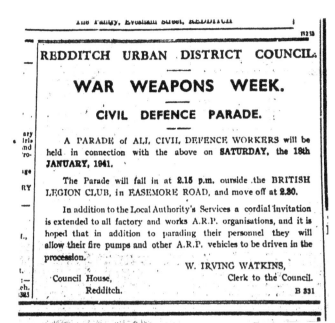

REDDITCH URBAN DISTRICT COUNCIL.

WAR WEAPONS WEEK.

CIVIL DEFENCE PARADE.

A PARADE of ALL CIVIL DEFENCE WORKERS will be held in connection with the above on **SATURDAY, the 18th JANUARY, 1941.**

The Parade will fall in at **2.15 p.m.** outside the BRITISH LEGION CLUB, in EASEMORE ROAD, and move off at **2.30.**

In addition to the Local Authority's Services a cordial invitation is extended to all factory and works A.R.P. organisations, and it is hoped that in addition to parading their personnel they will allow their fire pumps and other A.R.P. vehicles to be driven in the procession.

W. IRVING WATKINS,

Council House, Clerk to the Council.

Redditch. B 331

War Weapons Week was designed to boost morale and increase investment in War Bonds to make money available for the war effort. The parade included all Civil Defence units together with fire engines and ARP vehicles.

REDDITCH WAR WEAPONS BID AT FULL VOLUME

ALD. TERRY POINTS INFLATION MORAL : SOVEREIGN BOUGHT A MILLION MARKS

SIR JOHN WARDLAW-MILNE'S SPEECH AT OFFICIAL LUNCHEON

Colonel W.H. Wiggins addresses the assembled crowd in Church Green East.

During the month of September 1940, collections were made and these badges were sold in an attempt to raise enough money in the town to buy a Spitfire.

Redditch Indicator, Saturday 7 September 1940.

ITCH, SATURDAY, SEPTEMBER 7, 1940.

PUBLIC NOTICES.

THE SPITFIRE SPIRIT

HAS SPREAD THROUGHOUT THE TOWN AND DISTRICT.

Organisers have been appointed as follows :—

District and Section	Representative
STUDLEY & SAMBOURNE	C. Blick and J. Bennett.
BENTLEY	Mr. M. Rowles.
WEBHEATH	Mrs. Greenhall.
HAM GREEN	Miss Wilson, The Mill.
ASTWOOD BANK	Mr. Elleos, Avenue Road.
WYTHALL & WEATHEROAK	Mr. C. S. Yeomans, Silver Street, Wythall.
CRABBS CROSS	Mr. Warner, 411, Evesham Road.
BEOLEY	Mr. C. Ireson, " Lorette."
HEADLESS CROSS	Mr. E. E. Young and Mr. Poole.
ROWNEY GREEN	Mr. K. Simmons.
HUNT END	Mr. J. Hodson, Crabbs Cross Lane.
BORDESLEY	Mr. J. Owen, Bordesley.
ALVECHURCH	Mr. C. A. Bartleet, The Post Office.
TARDEBIGGE	Mr. Knight, The School House.
PECKENHAM	Mr. Frank Bradley.
SHOPS AND GARAGES	Mr. F. J. Dyer, Alcester Street.
LICENSED HOUSES	Redditch Licensed Victuallers' Association.
	Mr. L. Griffiths and Mr. H. Lawford.
FACTORIES	Mr. R. Bennett (Bennett Tools Ltd., Redditch)
	Mr. P. T. Austin (Redditch Indicator Co., Ltd.
COUNCIL HOUSE & YARD	Mr. Buckley, Surveyor's Department.
YOUTH CENTRE	Mr. Des James, Ipsley Street.
SCHOOLS	Mr. C. H. Blackford, J.P., C.C.
CINEMAS	Mr. A. E. White, Barclays Bank Ltd.
PROFESSIONAL HOUSES	Mr. J. Price, Bates Hill.
RAILWAY WORKERS	Mr. B. Marse.
THE POST OFFICES	Mr. F. Wright.

PLEASE CONTRIBUTE GENEROUSLY through your district, factory or other group. Lists will be published and badges issued next week. **IT IS HOPED TO BUY THE SPITFIRE BY SEPTEM-BER 30th—AND REDDITCH WILL IF EVERY-BODY DOES THEIR BIT.**

Subscriptions to Mr. A. E. WHITE, Treasurer, Barclays Bank.

General Enquiries of Mr. THOS. MARTIN, Hon. Secretary, Pool Place, Redditch. Telephone Redditch 500.

| REDDITCH URBAN DISTRICT COUNCIL. | REDDITCH METHODIST CHURCHES. DAY OF NATIONAL PRAYER. |

Redditch Indicator, Saturday 7 September 1940.

A Guard of Honour formed by 'C' Company of Redditch Home Guard being inspected by HRH the Duke of Kent outside the Select Cinema in Alcester Street on 27 February 1941. The Duke is talking to Leonard Preece whose brother, Bill, is present in the front rank.

HRH the Duke of Kent inspecting the Redditch Fire Brigade's three engines and crews. He is also talking to the Brigade commander, Mr L.O. Wilkes. The Duke was killed on 25 August 1942 when a Sunderland flying boat taking him to Iceland crashed into a Scottish mountainside, killing everyone on board except the rear-gunner.

KENT CONGRATULATES REDDITCH CIVIL DEFENCE PATRIOTISM

The Duke in conversation with Lieutenant Morom.

HRH Prince George, Duke of Kent.

The opening of Redditch community clubs by the Duchess of Kent, Thursday 4 December 1941. By 1941 about 4,000 extra workers had been imported into the town, the great majority were in lodgings and the clubs were set up to relieve the loneliness and boredom caused by wartime conditions.

At 29 Prospect Hill a Girls' Club was set up by the National Council of Girls' Clubs in cooperation with the Ministry of Labour Welfare Department. It was in the charge of Miss McLeary and provided a canteen, baths, laundry, rest rooms, emergency bedroom, games, sewing and other such amenities.

The Men's Club was across the road at 6 Prospect Hill, known as Fish Hill House. It was established by a local committee promoted by the Redditch and District Christian Council, supported financially by local firms, and it provided similar facilities for men. For joint activities about six halls in the town were available for men's, women's and mixed choirs, dances, whist drives, socials, entertainments, concerts and discussion groups.

Cricket XI — 1940–1941

Redditch County High School cricket team, 1940–1 season.

On arrival in Redditch HRH the Duchess of Kent was taken to the works of Herbert Terry & Sons Ltd, where she was met by a Guard of Honour from the company's Home Guard, which she inspected while being escorted by Captain Norman Terry. The party then proceeded to a reception in Terry's Welfare Hall where she met various local dignitaries.

Royal Enfield Football Club, 1941–2. With the Redditch League Shield and A.E. Memorial Cup. Back row: G.F. Appleyard, J. Goode, H. Payne, K. Grubb, N. Ralph, W. Wheeler, J. Yates. Front row: R. Biddle, A.E. Waite, F. Simons, J. Andrews, G. William, L. Kings, F. Wilkes.

THE MEN'S CLUB.

The Men's Club at the old 'Fish Hill House', 6 Prospect Hill.

THE GIRLS' CLUB.

The Girls' Club at 29 Prospect Hill.

3, South Street, Redditch, received information on Friday in last week that their son, Maurice V. Askew, R.A.F.V.R., was a prisoner of war, and on the following day they received a post card from him stating that he was quite well, and asking his parents not to worry. He was reported missing from air operations over Liepzig on the night of February 19th-20th, 1944.

Sergeant Askew joined the R.A.F.V.R. in December, 1939, and was called up for service in March. 1940. He became an air mechanic, and volunteered for flying duties, and passed as a flying engineer.

He was educated at St. Luke's School, Headless Cross, and the

Sergeant Maurice V. Askew, prisoner of war. Maurice Askew later emigrated to New Zealand where he and his wife still live.

(Below) With the young men of the town being 'called up' into the services and every other able-bodied man or woman employed in war work, staff shortages in other less vital jobs were inevitable.

TIMETABLE OF THE MAIN EVENTS OF THE SECOND WORLD WAR.

1939

September 1: Germany invades Poland.
September 3: Britain and France declare war on Germany.
September 17: Russia invades Poland.
September 29: Russia and Germany agree to divide Poland.

1940

April 9: Germany invades Denmark and Norway.
April 15: British troops land in Norway.
May 10: Germany invades Luxembourg, Holland and Belgium. Neville Chamberlain resigns and Winston Churchill becomes Prime Minister.
May 14: German forces invade France.
June 4: Dunkirk evacuation of British Expeditionary Force begins.
June 10: Italian dictator Mussolini declares war on the Allies.
June 25: France surrenders.
July 4: German Blitzkrieg on Britain begins.
August 13: Day of the Eagle operation by Luftwaffe marks the start of the Battle of Britain as 1,485 German aircraft cross the Channel.
October 12: Hitler cancels invasion plan for Britain and the Battle of Britain is won.

1941

January 5: North Africa campaign begins with UK attacks against Italian forces.
February 12: Rommel and Panzer formations arrive in Libya.
April 17: Yugoslavia falls to Germany.
May 2: Hess lands in Scotland.
June 22: Germany invades Russia.
October 6: German forces reach Moscow and Leningrad is besieged.
December 6: Counter-offensive by Russian forces and Germans retreat.
December 7: Japan enters the war with attack on American fleet at Pearl Harbour.
December 8: Japanese land in Malaya.
December 28: Historic first-ever raid by British commandos is launched successfully on Vaagso, Norway.

1942

January 15: Japan invades Burma.
February 15: Singapore surrenders.
May 26: Rommel attacks the British 8th Army in North Africa.
August 13: Montgomery takes command of the 8th Army.
October 23: Montgomery secures victory over Rommel at El Alamein.

1943

February 2: Germans surrender at Stalingrad.
May 13: Germans surrender in North Africa.
July 10: Allied invasion of Italy begins with landings on the Sicily coast.
July 25: Mussolini is overthrown.
September 9: Allied troops invade Salerno on the Italian coast.

1944

January 22: British and American troops land at Anzio.
June 4: Rome falls to the Allies.
June 6: D-Day ainvasion begins on the beaches of Normandy.
June 13: First V-1 bombs land on London.
July 20: Bomb plot against Hitler narrowly fails.
August 15: Allies invade the south of France.
August 20: Battle of Normandy ends with the closing of the Falaise Pocket. Advance to the River Seine begins.
August 25: Paris is liberated.
September 3: Brussels is liberated.
September 17-26: Operation Market Garden, the ``Bridge Too Far'' airborne mission to cross the Rhine at Arnhem, fails.
October 5: British forces land in Greece.
December 16: German offensive in the Ardennes region launches Battle of the Bulge.

1945

January 17: Russia forces capture Warsaw.
January 27: Auschwitz concentration camp is liberated by Russian troops and the full horrors of Nazi Germany are gradually revealed.
January 28: The final shots are fired in the Battle of the Bulge, giving victory to the Allies, but at a heavy cost in men and equipment.
February 13: RAF launches carpet bombing raid on Dresden, followed by three further raids by US Air Force.
April 12: President Franklin Roosevelt dies.
May 1: Adolf Hitler commits suicide in his Berlin bunker.
May 2: German forces in Italy surrender.
May 4: Montgomery receives surrender of German forces in Holland, north-west Germany and Denmark on the Luneberg Heath.
May 8: Victory in Europe Day (VE Day) as Field Marshal Keitel signs unconditional surrender in Berlin.
August 6: ``Little Boy'' atomic bomb is dropped on Hiroshima by US B-29 bomber Enola Gay.
August 9: ``Fat Man'' atomic bomb is dropped on Nagasaki.
August 15: Victory over Japan Day (VJ Day) as Emperor Hirohito announces unconditional surrender.

War Work in Redditch Factories

WITH THE outbreak of World War Two the industrial life of the town changed dramatically. The fishing tackle factories experienced a drop in demand for their peacetime products while firms like Royal Enfield were working flat out and expanding to meet the demands of the War Office.

New factories were built, old factories were switched to war work and the workforce retrained on a massive scale. Workers were urgently required to fill the new jobs and with the 'Call Up' taking the young men for active service, the women of Redditch took over their jobs and were aided by workers imported from other areas such as Wales.

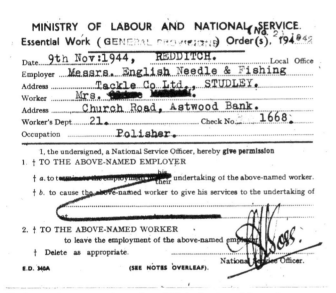

Regimentation was not just a fact of life in the Armed Forces but was extended to the civilian population as well. Even permission to leave or change jobs required application to a National Service Officer of the Ministry of Labour.

Girls of the Women's Land Army (and friends) celebrating Christmas at the Feckenham Hostel.

The Ministry of Labour also ran a poster campaign to persuade women to replace men in the factories.

The Women's Land Army parading through Redditch in a bid to raise 11,000 recruits.

The badge of the Women's Land Army.

WAR WORK'S TRUE STORIES, No 1

Marion finds a fighting job, too—

1. When Marion's boy-friend was called up, *she* wanted to be in it too. So she asked the Employment Exchange about War Work.

2. In next to no time they had fixed her up at a Government Training Centre, learning to make munitions.

3. And before long she was in an important war job. At last she felt she was really ' doing her bit."

4. Jim *was* proud of her when he came home on leave! He knows how much equipment counts in modern warfare!

There's War Work waiting for YOU! Go to your local office of the Ministry of Labour and National Service, they will tell you how best to serve your country.

Your duty now is

ISSUED BY THE MINISTRY OF LABOUR AND NATIONAL SERVICE

An appeal by the Ministry of Labour and National Service that appeared in the national press for women to work in factories to replace the men called into the armed services.

High Duty Alloys

'Never in the field of human conflict was so much owed by so
many to so few' – Prime Minister Winston Churchill.

IN THE YEAR proceeding World War Two the HDA parent company in Slough was at full stretch and it was obvious another factory would be needed. With financial help from the Bristol Aeroplane Company a dispersal shadow factory for a heavy forging plant was planned and Redditch was the site chosen, partially due to the close proximity of the gas works.

Work started on the 28 acre site in October 1938 and within 10 months the factory was fully operational without any Government support. Nevertheless, the factory was officially opened by the Secretary of State for Air, the Rt. Hon, Sir Kingsley Wood MP, on 16 August 1939. He set in

operation the giant Erie hammer, shipped over from America, the largest of its kind in Europe at that time. Bronze commemorative plaques by the sculptor Fred Kormis were given as mementos to guests. Three weeks later, on 3 September 1939, Great Britain and Germany were at war.

By 1940 the factory employed almost 2,000 people and turned out thousands of pistons, crank cases and airscrew blades every week – mainly for Rolls-Royce and Bristol engines – and billets for rolling and extrusion. Had it not been for the products of HDA, the wartime expansion of the RAF might have been delayed by up to a year and 'The Battle of Britain' could easily have been lost.

The site of High Duty Alloys factory in 1938 before building commenced.

The HDA factory nearing completion.

The factory was built on marshy ground and was prone to waterlogging, which was the cause of many construction problems.

The foundation for the Erie hammer consisted of a cylindrical hole 40ft in diameter and 40ft deep and into it was pumped 1,800 tons of concrete.

The 460-ton Erie hammer, known to all simply as 'The Big Hammer'. It had a forging weight of 29 tons and had been shipped in parts from America. It was off-loaded from the Thames docks and transported to Redditch by rail and road.

The Lancaster bomber powered by four Rolls-Royce Merlin engines using 48 pistons forged by HDA, who also made the mountings for the 'bouncing bombs' of the Dambusters' raid.

A post-war aerial photograph of the HDA factory in Windsor Road. The company is now known as Mettis Aerospace Ltd.

To mark the opening of the Redditch HDA factory on 16 August 1939 a copy of this bronze plaque, the work of sculptor Fred Kormis, was given to the more important guests at the ceremony.

The Supermarine Spitfire – Britain's most famous World War Two aircraft – contained parts made at HDA, Redditch.

World War Two badge worn by the ARP wardens at the Redditch HDA factory.

The victorious HDA 1942 football team – Redditch and District League Champions and winners of the COT Cup, a hospital charity.

Medal issued to HDA workers at Redditch in 1999 to commemorate the 60th anniversary of the opening of the factory.

The BSA Factory, Studley Road

ON 12 APRIL 1938, the War Office gave instructions to proceed with the building and equipping of a new factory in Redditch for the manufacture of the Besa machine gun. Within 14½ months the factory had been planned, built and put into operation and the first gun had been test fired.

The Studley Road factory site occupied 60 acres and work started immediately. About 70,000 tons of soil was moved to level the site and the building was ready to receive machinery by December 1938. The first of the workers began production in January 1939 and by June 320 people were being employed and sufficient progress had been made to enable one of the first batch of 50 guns to be completed and test fired on Tuesday 27 June.

When in full production the factory was designed to employ approximately 1,200 people including the office staff. Control and administration was from the parent company at BSA Works, Small Heath, Birmingham.

The basic principle of design of the Besa machine gun was the same as the Bren gun.

It was produced in two calibres, 7.92mm and 15mm, and was designed to give a very high performance – three thousand rounds could be fired in 30 minutes. It was later modified for use in tanks.

Levelling the site, 16 June 1938.

Under construction, 25 August 1938.

Some Interesting Facts About Manufacture

7.9 MM. GUN		15 MM. GUN	
Total number of machine operations	2,100	Total number of machine operations	2,200
Total number of hand operations	530	Total number of hand operations	630
Total number of Fixtures	1,150	Total number of Fixtures	844
Total number of Cutters	1,540	Total number of Cutters	1,730
Total number of Gauges	4,720	Total number of Gauges	4,947
Total number of parts in gun	110	Total number of parts in gun	110
Total weight of billets and forgings used for one gun . . . lbs.	232	Total weight of billets and forgings used for one gun . . . lbs.	697
Total weight of finished gun . lbs.	42	Total weight of finished gun . . lbs.	121
Total number of operations on miscellaneous parts (Remote Control, Ammunition Boxes, Cartridge Belt, Tools and Sundries)	590	Total number of operations on miscellaneous parts (Remote Control, Ammunition Boxes, Cartridge Belt, Tools and Sundries)	650

The Besa gun.

Rifling Machine used for Besa gun barrels.

Royal Enfield –
The Wartime Factories

AT THE outbreak of World War Two the whole of the Enfield Cycle Company's manufacturing output was concentrated at their old established works at Hewell Road, Redditch. Soon after the commencement of hostilities, however, it was found that expansion was necessary in order to cope with the quantity and variety of products required by the military authorities.

At the time of the collapse of France and the evacuation from Dunkirk the whole of the plant required for the manufacture of Royal Enfield Motor Mowers in Redditch was dismantled and stored outside the factory in order to provide space for manufacturing articles of national importance.

The space thus created was still not enough and it was not possible to extend the works in Redditch because of the shortage of skilled labour in the district. Satellite factories were therefore established in other parts of the country where labour was available or where suitable buildings already existed.

Eventually there were four factories established in different parts of England and Scotland and all worked in cooperation with one another.

No.2 Factory was established 90ft below ground in a disused Bath stone quarry at Westwood. It produced Predictors and ancillary equipment for range finding on Bofors and other guns.

No.1 Factory. Royal Enfield Cycle Company Head Office, Hewell Road, Redditch. The railway line is in the foreground. This is a retouched aerial photograph. The factory site covered 25 acres and was the chief centre for the production of motorcycles, bicycles, armour-piercing shot, oil motors, diesel engines and generator sets.

This prototype 348cc side valve, parallel twin motorcycle was purpose-built by Royal Enfield for the armed services.

Deep inside the disused Bath stone quarry at Westwood

No.3 Factory in Edinburgh made motorcycle frames and tubular crates to protect and contain airborne motorcycles (Flying Flea) when dropped by parachute.

No.4 Factory was in an old needle works in Feckenham a few miles from Redditch.

No.5 Factory in Redditch made use of part of Allcock's Fishing Tackle Standard Works. The Austin Motor Section was in another part of the same works.

A post-war picture of Royal Enfield's No.4 Factory at Feckenham.

Royal Enfield's production of bicycles and motorbikes was solely for military use. One of the developments was a lightweight 125cc bike known as the 'Airborne', which was able to be dropped by parachute for the use of airborne troops. This machine came to be known as 'The Flying Flea'.

Badges worn by workers at one of the Austin Aero Engines shadow factories in the area. The Austin shared part of Allcock's factory, as did the Royal Enfield.

Redditch factories were used to producing large needle shapes such as marlinspikes or bodkins for mattress making. During World War Two it is thought that a factory in the district, possibly Astwood Bank, was making the spike-type bayonets similar to the one illustrated.

Urgent War Munition Work

Several GIRLS and WOMEN

Wanted for Power Press Work

HERBERT TERRY & SONS, LTD.

REDDITCH.

Herbert Terry's advert in the newspaper on 1 June 1940.

Royal Enfield Football Team 1943–4. Back row: J. Yates, H. Nash, N. Ralph, R. Court. Middle row: O. Wythes, G. Appleyard, H. Payne, W. Wheeler, K. Grubb, A. Gregory, L. Sargeant, J. Roberts. Front row: G. Williams, R. Biddle, Major F.W. Smith, E. Court, J. Andrews, T. Benjamin (trainer). (Played 33, Won 33).

Ministry of Home Security Volunteer dispatch riders mounted on Royal Enfield Motor Cycles.

'The Flying Flea'.

Parachute and glider troops were equipped with Royal Enfield 125cc 'Airborne' Motor Cycles.

The Enfield Works Fire Brigade in the 'Salute the Soldiers' parade on Church Green West in aid of war savings.

The Royal Enfield Company of the 9th Battalion (Worcester) Home Guard.

During the War the Enfield Company produced for the Nation—

BICYCLES
Military Mark V and Civilian Types.

MOTOR CYCLES
(1) 125 c.c. for Paratroops and Airborne Regiments.
(2) 250 c.c.
(3) 350 c.c. } for Naval, Military, Royal Air Force and Civil Defence Services.
(4) 500 c.c.

PETROL-ELECTRIC GENERATOR SETS
(1) 80-watt Lightweight Charging Sets for distribution by Parachute.
(2) 2·75 K.V.A. Three-phase Sets for use on Bofors Gun Sites.
(3) Light Transportable Sets for operating Radar Stations.
(4) Multi-Generator Sets for testing Aircraft and Radar Equipment.

DIESEL-ELECTRIC GENERATOR SETS
5·6 K.V.A. Diesel-driven Generator Sets.

ELECTRIC-ELECTRIC GENERATOR SETS
Electrically-driven Generator Sets for testing Aircraft and Radar Equipment.

PREDICTORS
(1) No. 3, for use with Bofors Guns.
(2) No. 7, for use with 6-pounder Guns and incorporating the use of Radar for Range-finding.

OIL MOTORS
(1) For operating Bofors Guns.
(2) For controlling Naval Searchlights.
(3) For Ships' Stabilizers.
(4) Tandem Units for Coastal Artillery.
(5) Fuse-setting Units.

ARMOUR-PIERCING SHOT
For 40 m.m. Anti-tank Guns.

GYROSCOPIC SIGHTS
For Oerlikon and other Guns.

ANTI-VIBRATION MOUNTINGS
For Gun Sights.

PUMP UNITS
For operating the Gun Turrets of Tanks.

CAMS
Straight-line Cams for use in Precision Instruments where extreme accuracy is required.

GEAR CUTTING
Specialised Gears of all kinds for many different purposes.

MISCELLANEOUS COMPLETE UNITS
Resetter Boxes for Gun Sites.
Self-synchronising Equipment for 40 m.m. Guns.
Lag-compensating and Self-sectoring Equipment for Gun Sights.

DESIGNS AND PROTOTYPES
In addition to the above articles, which have been produced in quantities, the following have been designed and development work has been carried out on prototypes.
(1) 10 h.p. Air-cooled Diesel Engine.
(2) 500-watt Lightweight Generator Set.
(3) 600 V.A. Ultra-Lightweight Generator Set.
(4) 1,500-watt Generator Set.

ARMY.

Military Mark V Bicycles.

Two pounder armour piercing shot, made in Redditch.

Alkaline Batteries Factory, Union Street

THE STEEL Alkaline Battery played a major part in World War Two as its strength, reliability, long life, high performance and ability to withstand rough handling rendered it particularly suitable for many applications in connection with armaments. The wartime difficulties in obtaining raw materials for battery production – nickel salts, graphite, caustic potash, cadmium, iron with a low manganese content, rubber and many others – meant that the factory's Research and Development section was almost continually active, day and night throughout the war, finding substitutes and improvements which eventually found a permanent place in post-war products.

Production continued throughout the war with the factory escaping major damage by the enemy. There was, however, a disastrous fire in a section of the plant designed to produce 'nickel snow' near the Tool Room in September 1940. Much damage was caused by a large number of gas cylinders exploding like bombs and molten bitumen and lead solidifying in the drains. Many alkaline steel batteries were recovered from the debris and more than 90 percent were found to be in perfect condition. Less than three weeks after the fire, battery production recommenced.

Alkaline steel batteries were used in mines, torpedoes, anti-aircraft gun-firing, rocket firing, turret control, signaling, emergency lighting, buoys, radios, radar, searchlights, vehicles, beacon lights and many other military instruments.

The factory has had many changes of name over the years; starting off as simply Batteries Ltd in 1920, it became Nife Batteries Ltd, later Britannia Batteries and Pertrix then Alkaline Batteries which was later changed to Chloride Alcad.

Britannia Batteries, Lodge Road (Union Street) Factory. This section is the 1905 extension which was built when BSA took over from the Eadie Manufacturing Company.

Naval torpedo-carrying aircraft. The torpedoes were fitted with steel alkaline batteries.

Britannia Batteries Ltd, Redditch. Packaging sticker logo.

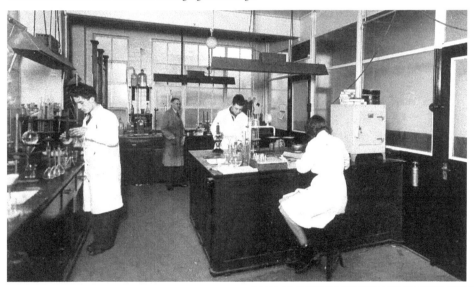

A photograph of one of the four laboratories that controlled the specification of the materials used in battery manufacture in order to ensure a long and trouble-free life.

A 1943 photograph of the Batteries workforce at the Lodge Road (Union Street) works. The battery powered 'Electricars' are lined up ready for export to Russia. The translation of the Russian wording is… WISHING SUCCESS AND QUICK VICTORY TO OUR RUSSIAN FRIENDS.

ЖЕЛАЕМ УСПЕХА И СКОРОЙ ПОБЕДЫ
НАШИМ РУССКИМ ТОВАРИЩАМ

The home of Britannia Batteries.

The area of the factory destroyed by the fire which broke out at 2.40am on 12 September 1940.

All-Steel alkaline tubular cell.

Directors and officials of Nife Batteries Hunt End factory together with the works Fire Brigade. The photograph appeared in the *Redditch Indicator* on Saturday 22 June 1940. Note the wartime camouflage painted on the wall of the factory.

Air Raids and the Blitz

'The growing power of the British bomber force is the herald of what Germany will receive, city by city from now on… German cities, harbours and centres of war production will be subjected to an ordeal the like of which has never been experienced by any country in continuity, severity or magnitude.'
(Extract from speeches by Prime Minister Winston Churchill on 1 and 2 of June 1942.)

DAYLIGHT probing raids by German Luftwaffe aircraft over-flying this area commenced in late July 1940 from captured airfields in Rennes in Brittany and Villacoublay in Normandy. In August the airfield at the Austin Aero Works at Cofton and Longbridge was attacked with extensive damage to tyre and petrol dumps, the columns of black smoke clearly seen from Redditch.

By September 1940, daylight reconnaissance raids were commonplace and uninterrupted, no doubt due to the fact that the RAF was otherwise engaged in 'The Battle of Britain' on the south coast. These raids, mainly by high flying Heinkels, Dorniers and JU 88s of Luftflot (Airfleet) 3, continued well into Autumn 1940 as a prelude to the Blitz of Birmingham and Coventry later in the year. Evidence of this, with Redditch as a 'centrepiece' target, is shown by the

Luftwaffe aerial photograph of the 'Britannia Battery Ltd' works, taken on 23 September 1940, and the subsequent events listed below:

1940

Friday night, 16 August (Unconfirmed report).
Incendiary bombs dropped on Redditch, Bromsgrove and other towns in Worcestershire.

Wednesday 2 October.
A HE (High Explosive) bomb was dropped on the town causing damage to 29 houses and the roof of the BSA factory canteen.

Thursday night, 22 October.
Another HE bomb and 50 incendiaries landed in Redditch. Bromsgrove and Evesham were also struck.

Saturday 9 November (Unconfirmed report).
Enemy aircraft machine-gunned the streets of several Midlands towns, including Redditch.

Tuesday 19 November.
Hundreds of enemy aircraft bombed Birmingham, in the final hours of the attack, six HE bombs were dropped at Washford causing damage to the bridge over the Arrow.

Friday 22 November.
Another major Birmingham raid with two HE bombs dropped at Rowney Green.

Wednesday 11 December
More Birmingham raids with damage to other Midlands towns. Redditch suffered its worst damage of the year. HE bombs caused death and damage in Orchard Street, Glover Street and Evesham Street. Six people were killed and 12 seriously injured, eight houses were demolished, 60 badly damaged and 178 partly damaged. In the town, 80 plate glass windows were broken. The Haywood Compressor Works (Hydrovane) also sustained damage. Bombs were also dropped on Wythall and Alvechurch and HE bombs on the nearby areas of Blackwell, Hanbury and Stoke Works.

1941

Wednesday 9 April
An HE bomb fell on the golf course and Redditch suffered a rain of incendiary bombs: over 1,000 were dropped from Bordesley to Batchley causing many small fires. Burcot, Wythall and Hollywood were similarly attacked.

Thursday 10 April
HE bombs fell on the area of Pitcher Oak Wood and at Barnt Green.

LATEST WAR NEWS.

FIVE DEAD IN TERROR RAIDS ON MIDLANDS.

RESCUE BID FOR TRAPPED SHELTERERS.

Ministry of Home Security communique issued this morning states that five people were killed and a number injured in enemy raids on the Midlands last night. In one Midland town in a sharp terror attack fires damaged commercial property and public buildings. High explosives hit houses, two public shelters, and a public house. A number of people were trapped in shelters and demolished houses, and rescue work has been begun. Bombs also fell in other Midlands areas, and a theatre was seriously damaged.

[Press Association message, 10.45 a.m., Friday.]

Over 3,000 vehicles are now running on home-produced fuel and the Minister of Mines is taking special steps to encourage the wider use of producer gas and other substitutes for petrol.

After the air raids of 2 and 22 October 1940, when HE bombs and incendiaries landed in the town, this small paragraph in the *Indicator* of Saturday 26 was all that was reported. Note that due to censorship no towns are named.

A photograph of Skinner's Buildings taken from Ipsley Street by the then 12-year-old Brian Danks. It shows the roof and window damage caused by the bombs dropped in nearby Kathleen Place and Orchard Street on the night of 11 December 1940. The man in the foreground is Bill Houghton.

Enemy raiders scattered bombs over a wide Midland area at night, and damage and casualties were reported from at least three towns. In one area a 'bus was hit; in others houses were wrecked, and there was one report of people trapped in a public shelter which suffered a direct hit. In one town considerable damage was done to dwelling houses and shop property, and several casualties, some of which proved fatal, occurred.

COOKHILL WOMEN'S INSTITUTE.

The Redditch Indicator of Saturday 14 December 1940 contained this report of the devastating bombing of the night of 11 December. Due to reporting restrictions imposed by censorship, no towns are named and only vague details of damage given. The last sentence probably refers to Redditch.

A local train driver tells the story that on the night of 11 December 1940, which was illuminated by bright moonlight, he was on the return journey from Birmingham when he saw a German bomber that appeared to be following his train and the railway line into Redditch. Where the line disappeared into the tunnel under Mount Pleasant the plane veered off to the left and dropped bombs on the town.

Partly as a result of the bombing and subsequent homelessness, World War Two saw the beginnings of the Redditch Citizens Advice Bureau. It was opened as a mobile unit and housed in a converted horsebox, aiming to help people cope with problems relating to war damage compensation, accommodation, evacuation, debt and even lost ration book. After the war the bureau closed down but was re-opened in the 1960s in a house on Peakman Street.

The deaths caused by the bombings on the night of 11 December 1940 appeared in the columns of the *Redditch Indicator* on the 21 December. The words 'passed away suddenly' and 'died suddenly' were all that the censor would allow.

AN open space in Glover Street, Redditch, created when the German bombs demolished two houses during the war, is to be the first children's playground to be established in the town by the Redditch Urban District Council.

Parents in that area are taking a keen interest in the scheme and on Wednesday evening they held a meeting at the Smallwood Almshouses to discuss what help they could give.

Councillor AE Taylor, who presided, gave an outline of the council's plans for the site and said that £600 had been set aside for the levelling of the ground and the purchase of equipment.

It was hoped to install a sandpit and various types of round-abouts

This painting by local artist Norman Neasom, who was part of the rescue team, depicts the air raid damage in Glover Street, Redditch, on the night of Wednesday 11 December 1940. Glover Street is in the foreground and in the background are the houses of Mount Street. The picture hangs in Redditch Town Hall and was commissioned by George White in 1941. The casualties were six killed and 36 injured. Several houses were destroyed and a large number suffered varying amounts of damage.

The wartime devastation in Glover Street is today replaced by the tranquillity of a children's play area.

Another of Norman Neasom's graphic illustrations showing the rescue party searching the rubble in Glover Street after the devastating air raid of Wednesday 11 December 1940. The backs of the houses in Mount Street are on the left with Marsden Road centre and right. The rescue team included Harry Jakeman, Albert Crow, Ernie Harris and Gilbert Batson.

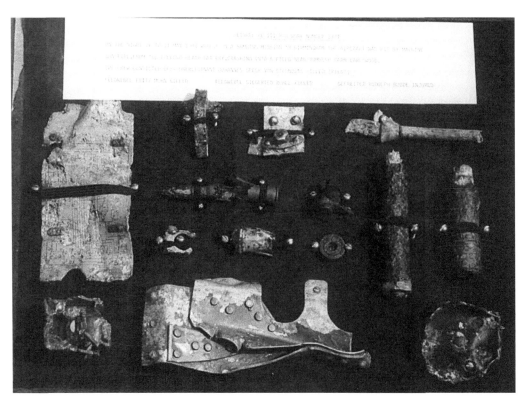

Items recovered from a German Heinkel HE111 shot down by the Fulford Heath Battery in a field at Rumbush Farm, Earlswood, on the night of 10 May 1941. The pilot was killed outright causing the plane to crash, killing the observer and the flight engineer with only the wireless operator surviving.

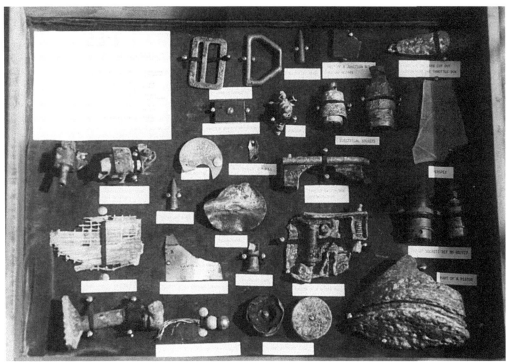

Parts recovered from a crash site at Lower Park Farm, Rowney Green. On 11 November 1943 a Wellington bomber overshot his run into Pershore Airfield. While the pilot was making a stall turn the port engine failed, causing him to lose control of the aircraft which then crashed, killing the crew of five. They were all from the Royal Canadian Airforce training centre at Pershore and are buried in the town cemetery.

Piece of shrapnel from Headless Cross. The large piece is part of the case of a bomb dropped by a German plane being chased off after a raid on Birmingham. It landed in fields near Mason Road and killed a pen full of chickens belonging to Mr Duggins. The small piece is from an AA shell, which hit the drainpipe of a house in the Meadway.

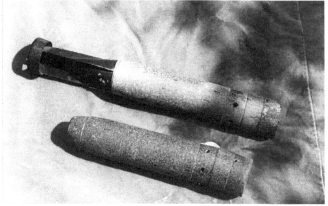

German incendiary bombs.

Wreckage from a British Beaufighter 11F which, on 15 November 1943, suffered instrument failure in a snowstorm causing the pilot to lose control. The aircraft flew low over a hill, hit a tree and crashed in a field at the rear of Shurnock Court near Feckenham, killing both members of the crew.

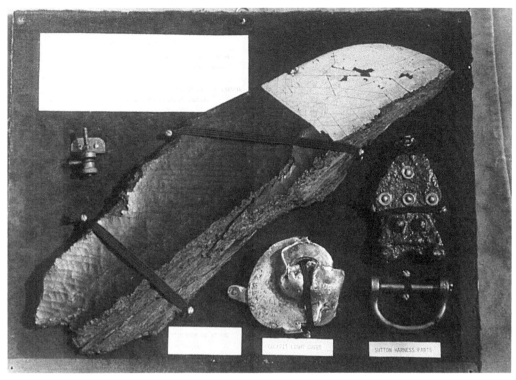

On Wednesday 9 April 1941 an HE bomb and several hundred incendiaries were dropped on the town. On the following Saturday the local newspaper devoted 3½ lines to the event.

The local council felt that it was necessary to give demonstrations to the general public on the workings of the stirrup pump. It would appear from the wording of this public notice that the council also sold the pumps.

Wartime Carnivals

1942 Redditch Carnival Queen Miss Beryl Martin in patriotic dress as 'Britannia' receiving the town key from Councillor J. Hughes on 8 August.

Britannia Batteries prize-winning float in a wartime Redditch Carnival.

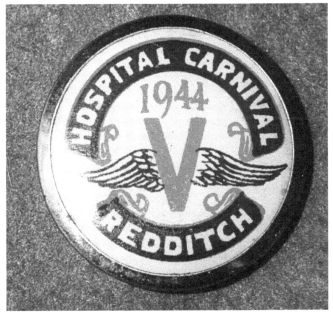

The 1944 Redditch Carnival raised funds for Smallwood Hospital. Among the special attractions was a 'Mile of Pennies', Bowling for a Live Pig on the Hospital Lawn and the Comedy Trick Cyclists 'two performances each day in front of the Hospital'.

The 1943 Carnival King and Queen, Arthur Swain and Barbara Lealand, on their way to Smallwood Hospital.

The 1944 Redditch Carnival Queen Miss Millicent Phillips and her attendants.

Victory

Many of the people in the crowd in this picture are holding the Order of Service hymn sheet that is also reproduced here (right).

VICTORY IN EUROPE PROCLAIMED
HOW REDDITCH RECEIVED THE GREAT NEWS

Redditch Indicator on Saturday 12 May 1945 showing the open air service on Church Green during which the Prime Minister's speech was relayed to the crowd.

Redditch Urban District Council

CIVIC SERVICE

ON CHURCH GREEN, REDDITCH TO COMMEMORATE THE CESSATION OF HOSTILITIES IN EUROPE

CHAIRMAN	Councillor J. H. TAYLOR, J.P. (Chairman of the Council).
OPENING SENTENCES	Rev. L. BRADLEY, M.A. (Vicar of Redditch).
HYMN	"Now thank we all our God."
PRAYER—Thanksgiving	Rev. L. BRADLEY, M.A.
HYMN	"Praise my soul, the King of Heaven."
PRAYER—Repentance	Rev. W. L. DOUGHTY, B.A., B.D. (Superintendent Minister Methodist Church).
HYMN	"O God, our help in ages past."
PRAYER—Amendment	Rev. E. L. PHILLIPPO (Vicar of St. George's, Redditch).
THE LORD'S PRAYER	
RESOLUTION—I promise, GOD helping me, to fight daily against my sins and to serve GOD more faithfully for JESUS' sake. Amen.	
BENEDICTION	
NATIONAL ANTHEM	

The Order of Service for the Civic Service held to commemorate the end of the war in Europe.

Mount Street VE Day peace celebrations. *Redditch Indicator* on 2 June 1945.

Marsden Road, VE Day celebration 1945.

8th June, 1946

To-day, as we celebrate victory, I send this personal message to you and all other boys and girls at school. For you have shared in the hardships and dangers of a total war and you have shared no less in the triumph of the Allied Nations.

I know you will always feel proud to belong to a country which was capable of such supreme effort; proud, too, of parents and elder brothers and sisters who by their courage, endurance and enterprise brought victory. May these qualities be yours as you grow up and join in the common effort to establish among the nations of the world unity and peace.

George R.I.

This card signed by the King was given to all school children as a memento of the war.

Celebrations in Britten Street, VE Day May 1945.

This photograph of Britten Street VJ Day party outside Holyoake's Field Wesleyan Methodist Mission Hall, Elm Road, appeared in the *Redditch Indicator* on Saturday 20 October 1945.

THE QUEEN, MISS EILEEN EAVES.

From the *Redditch Indicator*, Saturday 8 September 1945. The picture shows Mr J.H. Taylor JP, Chairman of Redditch Urban District Council and Mr C.H. Blackford laying the first post-war brick in Batchley Estate. The foundations of these houses were commenced in 1940 but owing to the wartime shortage of labour, the contract could not be completed.

The Redditch Victory Carnival on 15 September 1945. The Carnival Queen, Miss Eileen Eaves, is on her float in Alcester Street.

PUBLIC NOTICES.

Redditch Victory Carnival

SEPTEMBER 8th to 15th.
CARNIVAL DAY SEPTEMBER 15th.

Crowning Ceremony September 8th, at 4.45 p.m.

Dances and many other attractions each evening.
Twelve hours of Fun and Spectacle on Carnival Day.
THE LARGEST PROCESSION IN THE MIDLANDS.
Classes for All.　　No Entry Fees.　　Valuable Prizes.
GREAT VICTORY TABLEAU
with Carnival Queen and her Court.
Several Bands and the principal Jazz Bands of the Midlands, with many displays.
GIGANTIC FUN FAIR IN THE STREETS.
"SPLASH NIGHT," WEDNESDAY, SEPTEMBER 12th.

Do not forget your Souvenir Carnival Programme of week's Events. Also your Immunity Badge.

All enquiries to Hon. Secretary.
Carnival Headquarters, Beech House, Redditch.
B521

CARNIVAL VICTORY CONCERT
MONDAY NEXT,
County High School, Redditch, at 7.45 p.m.

Difficulties of a "Demob"

This post-war advert shows that even Kellogg's All-Bran played its part in getting the population 'back to normal'.

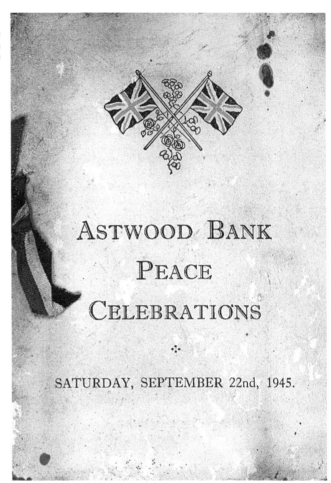

ASTWOOD BANK PEACE CELEBRATIONS

SATURDAY, SEPTEMBER 22nd, 1945.

In the afternoon the village held a fancy dress competition, a procession, tea and sports. In the evening there were entertainments in the Baptist School, a torch light procession and a bonfire with fireworks. At night there was a dance in the Church Room.

HOW MUCH COAL HAVE YOU HAD?

You may not obtain, except by licence from the Local Fuel Overseer, more than 10cwt. of coal (including Coalite) during the two months' period January-February, 1946, AND YOU CANNOT HAVE THAT AMOUNT if it would make your total supplies exceed the maximum of 50cwt. for any premises for the 12 months 1st May, 1945—30th April, 1946.

Whether you will be able to have the full 10cwt. even if that does not make your total exceed 50cwt. depends on the supply position. Supplies have been short and will have to be shared as fairly as possible among consumers.

The maximum total supply of coke, anthracite, Welsh dry steam coal and manufactured fuels other than coalite, again subject to supplies being available, is 20cwt. during the 6 months 1st November, 1945—30th April, 1946.

IF IN DIFFICULTY THROUGH NO FAULT OF YOUR OWN, apply to your Local Fuel Overseer, whose address can be obtained at any Post Office.

SAVE ALL THE FUEL YOU CAN— IN YOUR OWN INTEREST

Issued by the Mini...

Shortages of food and fuel continued for a long time after the cessation of hostilities as shown by this public notice dated 26 January 1946.

A booklet issued to all Service personnel on demobilisation at the end of hostilities. It dealt with early release, gratuities, employment, vocational training, grants, disablement pensions, etc.

The programme for the state procession, led by the royal family, giving the order of march of the armed forces and a list of 13 types of aircraft in the accompanying fly-past. It also gives details of the evening entertainments. This was, of course, taking place in London, but similar, smaller-scale celebrations occurred in every town and village in the country.

VJ Day party in Rookery Road, Headless Cross – now part of the Meadway.

Photograph published in the *Redditch Indicator* on Saturday 17 November 1945, showing five-year-old Dawn Hill planting an oak tree on Church Hill, assisted by Mr Corfield, Head Gardener at Beoley Hall, as part of the Beoley VJ celebrations.

World War Two
Bentley Manor's Last Days

SHORTLY AFTER the outbreak of World War Two in 1939 most of the Manor was commandeered by the Government and it became the headquarters of the local 267th Field Battery, Royal Artillery. Later the Essex Regiment took over the property and about 3,000 troops were billeted in and around the Manor. The Royal Engineers followed them and it later housed US troops, white and coloured units in turn. Towards the end of the war it was used as a prisoner of war camp with Germans and Italians interned there. Finally it accommodated displaced European nationals.

When the Manor was returned to the family, due to its greatly deteriorated condition and the discovery of extensive 'dry rot' infecting the timbers, the new owner Lieutenant Colonel Gray-Cheape was unable to occupy the property. It was offered to several possible purchasers but no one would undertake responsibility for it and the main building was demolished in 1950.

Bentley Manor 1906.

Bentley Manor today. The only buildings of Bentley Manor left standing are two potting sheds.

Memorials

BRIDGE STREET SCHOOL
WAR MEMORIAL UNVEILED BY ALDERMAN TERRY

Pupils and staff of Bridge Street School assembled for the unveiling of the war memorial sundial.

A war memorial was erected in the grounds of Bridge Street school in July 1946, dedicated to the memory of 19 former pupils and one assistant master who perished in World War Two. It was unveiled by Charles Terry JP.

Redditch War Memorial outside St Stephen's Church. The names of those who fell in World War One appear on the top panels and those who fell in World War Two around the base.

ND - #0373 - 270225 - C0 - 297/210/8 - PB - 9781780913483 - Gloss Lamination